HIDDEN TREASURES

WESTERN KENT

Edited by Lynsey Hawkins

First published in Great Britain in 2002 by
YOUNG WRITERS
Remus House,
Coltsfoot Drive,
Peterborough, PE2 9JX
Telephone (01733) 890066

All Rights Reserved

Copyright Contributors 2002

HB ISBN 0 75433 902 5
SB ISBN 0 75433 903 3

FOREWORD

This year, the Young Writers' Hidden Treasures competition proudly presents a showcase of the best poetic talent from over 72,000 up-and-coming writers nationwide.

Young Writers was established in 1991 and we are still successful, even in today's technologically-led world, in promoting and encouraging the reading and writing of poetry.

The thought, effort, imagination and hard work put into each poem impressed us all, and once again, the task of selecting poems was a difficult one, but nevertheless, an enjoyable experience.

We hope you are as pleased as we are with the final selection and that you and your family continue to be entertained with *Hidden Treasures Western Kent* for many years to come.

CONTENTS

Borough Green Primary School

Caroline Baker	1
Marcus Greening	1
Emily Dibble	2
Callum McCloskey	2
Chris Smith	3
Cherrie De-Kisshazy	4
Laura Porter	4
Jade Lambert	5
Helen Dann	5
Bethany Dunmore	6
Joshua Gordon	6
Jessica Minnis	7
William Martin	8
Laura Reeves	8
David Chapman	9
Rebecca Swann	10
Joanna O'Connor	10
Katie Gillard	11
Daniela Pasquini	12
Kirstie Keable	12
Sarah Guest	13
Nicholas Burton	14
Hannah Cross	14
Russell McEwan	15
Kahn Cooper	16
Alexandra Saunders	16
Scott Treleaven	17
Thomas Hinkin	17
Ryan Wyatt	18
Florence Bailey	18
Bob Entwistle	19
Catriona Rowbury	20

Cage Green Primary School

Jamie Cutts	20
Amy Pyne	21
Anna-Marie Buckley	21
Matthew Derrick	22
Grace Dugdale	23
Laura Pullen	24
Tonya Streeter	24
Emma Saunders	25
Annabel Marriott	25
Sophie Thompson	26
Tarn McGibbon	26
Ellisha Owen	27
Sophie Littlechild	27
Rebecca Eldridge	28
Sam Wesley	28
Stephanie Bradley	29
Nicholas Carlton	30
Franki Gower	30
Nicola Wood	30
Jess Owen	31
Alice Plummer	31
Stuart Obbard	32
Jamie Bott	32
Emma Gray	32
James Burton	33
Hayley Francis	33
Matthew Evans	34
Naomi Glazier	34
Vicky Cole	35
Josef Hills	35
Robyn Morris	36
Kristy Dugdale	36
Charlotte Coulter	37
Jamie Matheson	37
Lauren Goad	38
Amber Page	38
Jack Powell	39

Martyn Pyne	39
Abby Jeffery	40
Hayley Eldridge	40
Brogan Hook	41
Emma Kirkpatrick	41
Joshua Moor	42

Clare House Primary School

Jack Everitt	42
Olivia Holmes	43
Madalen Weeks	44
James Jarratt	44
Hannah Caswall	45
Hannah Jaroudy	45
Harriet Dempsey	46
Yasmin Hatfield	46
Sam Smith	47

Downe Primary School

Hannah Page	47
Michael Lever	48
Danielle Leonard	48
Adam Young	49
Erin Gilbrook	50
Jack Jeffrey	50
Samuel Davey	50
Charlie Matthews	51
Sam Garwood	51
Ryan Sadler	52
Jack Jewell	52
Karla Sikora	53

Hildenborough CE Primary School

Robyn Willard	53
Hamish De Rusett	54
Patrick Duckworth	55
Katy Richardson	56
Amy Cowlard	57

	Phoebe Cattley	57
	James Denman	58
	Richard Hughes	58
	Mark Pratt	59
	Leo Hall	60
	Jessica Gibbs	60
	Naomi Whittome	61
	Andrew Taylor	61
	Dolly Kershaw	62
	Victoria Keegan	62
	Max Richards	63
	Rebecca Jenkins	64
	Emily Miller	64
	Elizabeth Berry	65
	Kirsty Coles	66
	Eleanor Edwards	66
	Matthew Watts	67
	Jack Witcomb	68
	Luke Hardy	68
	Nicholas Kennedy	69
	Laura Southall	70
	Jak Cook	70
	Jade Williams	71
	Maxwell Oakley	71
	Natasha Wood	72
	Michael Denton	72
	Sam Brown	73
Marden Primary School		
	Bethany Thomas	74
	Victoria Keith	74
	Jamie Sancto	75
	Jonathan Funnell	75
	James Boys	76
	Richard Osborne	76
	Christian Hindley	77
	Alex Excell	77
	Ruth Kelly	78

Platt CE Primary School
	Rheanna Woodman	78
	Leigh-Anne Reardon	79
	Stephanie Lee	79
	Class D	80
	Joseph Gallant	81
	James Wagstaff	81

St Anselms RC Primary School, Dartford
	Keiran Yates	82
	Daniel Brooks	83
	Matthew Linnett	84
	Joshua Perry	84
	Samuel Whapshott	85
	Ruaidhri Marshall	86
	Aaran Silva	86
	Tom Marsh	87
	Louis Crowley	88
	Hayley Wilkinson	88
	Stephen Hutchins	89
	Sian Bull	90
	Emmanuel Ahamefula	91
	Laura Harney	92
	Celina Quinn	93
	Emma Pearce	94
	Lara Wrubel	95
	Kevin Coen	96
	Bethany Campbell	97
	Siobhan Martin	98
	James Aylwin	99
	Miriam Adisa	100
	Gregory White	101
	Sophie Randall	102
	Kelvin Canty	102

St James' RC Primary School, Bromley
	Hannah Williams	103
	Matthew Pettifer	104

Louise Allen	104
Thomas Eves	105
Luke Brook	106
Rachel Allen	106
Charles Turner	107
Joshua Hughes	108
Ruth Andrews	109
Nicholas Greenwood	110
Harry McAleer	110
Charlotte Georgina Weeks	111
Molly Grace Fathers	111
Grace McCarthy	112
Jack Harper	113
John Hatch	114
Robert Adams	114
Liam Docherty	115
Leo Wyard	115
Emily Hobbs	116
Patrick Bunnage	117
Dominic Makepeace	118
Roberto Battista	119
Catherine Preston	120
Emily Loftus	120
Marie Wallis	121
John Pereira	122
Taylor Norman	122
Stephanie Arch	123
Amy Ewen	124
Charlotte Rafferty	124
Hannah Meadowcroft	125
Niall Wharton	125
Rebecca Reidy	126
Rachel Pritchard	126
Catherine Dow	127
Simon Brindley	127
Rachel Baldwin	128
Kelly-Ann Marrington	129
Jessica Watkins	130

Joe Hall	130
Joelle O'Neill	131
Daniel Brindley	132
Thomas Knight	133
Alex Dumbrell	134
Niall Slater	134
Jack Hughes	135
Rebecca Powell	136
Laura Lee	137
Jenny Sharpe	138
Charlotte Morgan	138
Katherine Lee	139
Ciaran O'Mahony	140
Pippa Cawley	141
Joseph Murray	142
Charlotte Dickinson	142
James Sutch	143
Lucy Hobbs	144
Jacob Cleveland	145
Cassie Cava	146
Daniel Hobbs	147
John Griffin	148
Nina Smyth	148

St Joseph's RC Primary School, Dartford

Jodie Mackerill	149
Mostafa Abdel-Kader	149
Ciara Smith & Sophie Kulczycki	150
Suzie Turrell	151
Hannah Daniels	151
Lhiane Jenner	152
Andrea Regan	152
Megan Smith	153
Rebecca Farrell	154
Maria Bull	154
Amy Leung	155
Rhiannon Bernard	155
Maria Wall	156

Louise Nathanielsz	156
Jessica Moles	157
Kayleigh O'Connell	157
Roisin Young	158
Nicola Seal	158
Jade Easton	159
Katrina Groves	159
Harriet Butler-Ellis	160
Tasha Young	160

Sevenoaks Prep School

Natasha Hamilton-Brown	160
Winston Surrey	161
Steen Tranholm Reed	161
William Ritchie	162
Mike Higgs	163
Mark Lucas	163
Raffaella Buck	164
Paul Boles	164
Ben Regan	165
Charlotte Smith	165
Harriet Partridge	166
Jonny Drown	166
Anthony Kayne	167
Tarra Nichols	167
William Harris	168
Vincent Post	168
Andrew McDowall	169
Amy Salt	170
Edward Cloke	170
Kassim Ramji	171
Kathryn Dendias	172
Zoe Montanaro	172
Alice Bramall	173
Michael Tynan	174

Sussex Road CP School
- Jason Carver — 174
- Joshua Lincoln — 175
- Amy Munday — 175
- Jonathan Nazer — 176
- Samuel Truscott — 176
- Nicola Drew — 177
- Andrea Sargent — 177
- Lauren Rickard — 178
- Emma Gilham — 178
- Nicole Standage — 179
- Ben Woods — 179
- Robert Jackson — 180
- Adam Hammond — 180
- Tyler Dunlop — 181
- Robert Fenwick — 181
- Sophie Warnett — 182
- Luke Webber — 182
- Luke Chatfield — 182
- Matthew Rutch — 183
- Jamie Curtis-Jones — 183

Southborough Primary School
- Lauren Knight — 184
- Sarah Bristow — 185
- Laura Blackman — 186
- Wemimo Onashoga — 186
- Samantha Martin — 187

The Brent CP School
- Paige Sutherland & Amy Kither — 188
- Donna Constant — 188
- Harrison Roberts — 189
- Daniel Jervis — 189
- Daniella Diaz-Bates — 190
- Craig Wiltshire — 190
- Jenny Haines — 191
- Carrie-Ann Shine — 191

	Kiran Khattra	191
	Rachel Pooley	192
	Daniel Russell	192
	William Moore	192
	Karen Smith	193
	Samantha Railton	193
	Nicholas Mills	193
	Holly Ingram	194
	Broden Ajgarni	194
	Daniel Phillips	194
	Laura Ross	195
	Tommy Hutchinson	195
	Toby Santinella	195
	Lucy Grant	196
	Jaz Key	196
Weald CP School		
	Laura Asplin	196
	Thomas Cochrane-Powell	197
	Charlotte Vile	198
	Emily Kerr	199
	Suzanne Howe	200
	Charlotte Jarvis	200
	Bridget Miller	201
	Hannah Goozee	201
	Robert Cooper	202
	Samantha Holloway	202
	Lucy Hall	203
	Heather Olley	203
	Sophie Lamb	204
	Hannah Whitbourn	204
	William Fauchon-Jones	205
	Francesca Lee	205
	Laura Virgo	206
	Samuel Jones	206
	Susannah Martin	207
	Christopher Jones	207
	Helen Smart	208

Christopher Ryan	208
Eleanor Jones	209
James Stout	209
James Dennison	210
Mary Griffiths	210
Robert Stone	211

West Malling CE Primary School

Samuel Holyhead	211
Chantelle Capeling	212
Ryan Webb	212
Jade Thompson	212
Rebecca Burr	213
Alexandra Gridley	213
Samantha James	214
Christina Theophanides	214
Azim Sobrany	215
Joshua de Gray	215
Sammi-Jo Lawrence	216
Jake Smith	216
Deanne Soules	217
Marcus Towner	217
Ben Greenwood	218
Katherine Styance	218

The Poems

FIRE

Here she comes gleaming and flickering,
Shh, be careful, she's prowling through your trodden path,
Striped like a shimmering tiger
With colours of glowing orange
And turquoise-green.
Quick, run if you've been seen
The silent daisy in its chosen pathway, is carried by its roaring flame,
This carnivorous creature is one that cannot be tamed.
The beastly, empty animal is always alert,
Ready to eat you -
Believe me it will hurt.
It's too much for a couple of stars,
The others already have damaging scars,
But the talented hunters have sought her,
And now she's saturated
And she hasn't mated.
There's not a single newborn, shining spark in sight,
In this fire!

Caroline Baker (9)
Borough Green Primary School

FIRE

Here comes the great acrid hedgehog,
Smouldering and burning,
Spitting embers and roaring,
Spines ignited,
Legs smouldering,
Dancing angrily in the shocking orange flames,
Jumping like mad about and staring at me,
From the red flames of the warm coal fire,
In my humble kitchen.

Marcus Greening (9)
Borough Green Primary School

A Borough Green Winter

On a cold, frosty and glacial morning,
A faint, weak sun battles against the dark, ugly clouds
Desperate to shine in the dull, misty sky.
Down below, trees stand not quite bare,
Raindrops cling to the moss-covered branches,
Already buds can be seen bursting forth
Becoming new spring leaves and early blossom.
On the school playground the netball stands
Look like statues frozen to the ground.
In the distance a neat row of houses
Tower above the meadow
With windows with crying eyes
Looking at the forthcoming life.
In the meadow a flock of birds
Break the silence with their cheerful chatter,
Occasionally a single bird flits across the sky,
Racing the slow-moving grey clouds.
Suddenly a huge flock of birds leave the meadow,
They struggle against the long, damp wind.
The distant tops of tall buildings are hidden
In a cold, thick mist.
On the icy, slippery doorsteps of distant houses,
Frozen milk stands proudly,
The summer days have fallen like the leaves of a winter's tree.

Emily Dibble (10)
Borough Green Primary School

A Borough Green Winter

Frost-bitten cars lay dead in the car park,
As a slow trundling train slithers on its paralleled path.

A leafless tree stands swaying in the harmless wind,
As windows from houses glare onto the damp, smelly field.

A flock of birds sings cheerfully all perched on a tree,
As frozen children enter their warm, humble classrooms.

Raindrops sliding onto branches of trees,
That's what it's like for a winter in Borough Green.

Callum McCloskey (9)
Borough Green Primary School

A TUDOR AUTUMN

As the icy wind blows
The rickety windmill spins gradually.

A feeble farmer is ploughing his extensive field
Holding his back because of the exhausting work.

In the sky elegant birds are flying through the autumn trees,
Meeting friends to migrate.

A single golden leaf falls and lands in the motionless river,
The crescent river is calm and gentle.

Beyond the orange trees are burly grave diggers
Digging with their shabby shovels.

The quaint farmer is looking after his healthy crops,
The indigo sky is getting darker.

Wheat, barley, corn and oats stand proudly,
The ground is being dug up by the Tudor plough.

Finally peasant work is done,
The farmer can rest in his peasant cottage,
After this busy autumn day.

Chris Smith (10)
Borough Green Primary School

THE WRITING OF MY POEM

As the clock chimes midnight
The fire is smouldering,
Presents wait to be revealed
To excited children.
Stockings bulge like Santa's wide belt
After a tasty Christmas meal.
The last square on the advent calendar
Will be happily opened tomorrow.
Grandad is snoring lazily in the armchair,
His newspaper sitting still over his bald head.
Lights cascade down the wall,
Twinkling like bright stars.
The voices of carol singers can be heard
Singing peaceful and calm from in the distance.

Cherrie De-Kisshazy (9)
Borough Green Primary School

WINTER

Beyond the deceased, bitter, frigid land
Whilst trees sway, oscillate, drowse as they stand,
Our lord, the monarch, our king comes by
Finally he bellows and roars a sigh.
Below the fleecy, silky, smooth sky,
No comfortable feeling is high.
When we're all ready for a cooked up steak
Upon the smooching, leaping, twirling wind,
A single leaf stumbles, tumbles, falling on the wind.
Winter's bitter, winter's frosty,
Winter's glacial, winter's draughty.

Laura Porter (10)
Borough Green Primary School

THE WEIRD DEAD PLANT

This antediluvian object,
Is from Australia.
It sits on my temperate fire
Its leaves are bushy like an intellectually tree at the top
It's like my brother's footballs I just want to run up and kick it.
I told my dad it looks very strange
And to take it back to the weird place where it came from.
It's brown with leaves that look dead as a dinosaur
It's seen me and my brother fight, it's been through two Christmases.
It's seen the snow and the leaves falling off the trees
It's seen the bright yellow sun beaming through the window.
My dad got it from his dad
Mum didn't like it so she hid it behind a pot of flowers
That's my weird dead plant!

Jade Lambert (10)
Borough Green Primary School

TUDOR POEM

In the autumn children are throwing rotten apples
At the people in the stocks.
Peasant women wear short dresses,
Wheat, barley and corn
An old woman sits in the ducking stool
Being punished.
Sheep are in the fields,
Behind, the homes sit on the hills.
The mill is grinding corn,
The birds fly to the trees
To migrate.
The leaves drop in the cold river,
Children play marbles and hool-a-hoops.

Helen Dann (9)
Borough Green Primary School

A Borough Green Winter

What can I hear?
Wait, birds chirping happily about the day,
A tree stands dead still
With its antler branches drifting back and forth.
A single dainty raindrop drops one by one,
The shabby, dented bark is chipping off the old trees
Ready to have a cheerful, new, brown coat.
While the evergreens rub their upright leaves.
The pale blue sky changes overhead, it's covering up the moonlight sun
With the marshmallow clouds.
The sky changes from a boring grey to a burnished blue,
The slithering snake of a train whizzes past, red, blue and yellow,
The wet ground rough, mild lays there asleep,
Houses overlook the silent field with their glaring eyes watching me as
I walk past.
The perspiring wood is all shabby and damp
Soon it will be spring at school.

Bethany Dunmore (9)
Borough Green Primary School

Snow

Snow sprinkled its white, flaky powder
Making the whole world's surface white
Children played as it sieved the powdery substance
Through its colossal hands.

It picked some up and blew it into a blizzard
Everyone scattered as the blizzard blew
When the blizzard stopped the children came out to play.

The children had a snowball fight
And the snow joined in
But then it cried big tears because he lost
It flooded the whole world with its tears.

Joshua Gordon (11)
Borough Green Primary School

COLOURS OF CHRISTMAS

Christmas is red . . .
A bauble is hanging next to a very poor bauble all
                                                           cracked and smashed,
A pudding is being made with icing to decorate its dull look,
Children pull a cracker with matching hats and toys,
Houses are filled with ribbons and wrapping paper
And tinsel hangs from the ceiling.

Christmas is green . . .
A baby is born called Jesus who is wrapped in swaddling clothes,
Kings come with green robes expecting to be bowed to,
The inn keeper comes with a lantern which shines out green light,
Angels come with green presents which sparkle in the night,
And with a sparkle of glitter baby Jesus is strong enough to
                                                                do anything.

Christmas is white . . .
A huge, white blanket covers the world,
Icicles fill the houses with chills,
Snowmen dance on the magical night,
Decorations are hung mostly of white
And children play dressing up in white.

Jessica Minnis (8)
Borough Green Primary School

WITCHES WOOD

We didn't see witches
In Witches Wood
But we saw where the witches had been
Where the witches had been
We saw where the witches had wrestled a tiger
That could have only been shot with
Witches' magic powers.

We saw the witch's hat
Where it had fallen off
When fighting the tiger
We saw lying on the ground
The witch's hair
Still knotty and scrawny.

We didn't see witches
In Witches Wood
But this was the closest
We'd ever been
To believing.

William Martin (7)
Borough Green Primary School

WIND

Swirling round the autumn trees
Picking up the colourful leaves
Breathing on the world below
The people get cold and have to go.

Now his friends have all gone home
He's sad as now he's all alone
Calling out to those he loves
Waking up the Heaven above.

He goes home and starts to cry
On his way he whispers goodbye
He thought, why couldn't they all stay?
Oh well I'll go back another day.

Laura Reeves (11)
Borough Green Primary School

SNOW

The snow attacked the trees
As it fell on its long journey.
It twisted and twirled,
Danced and pranced,
Before lying still on the frosty ground.

It ate into my flesh
As I trudged along.
It coated my hand
With a layer of coldness.
It whipped my face.

It whistled down the chimney
And crackled as it landed in the fire.
The wind pushed it on,
And it went,
Screaming and swirling past the window.

It soared past the trees,
Coating them in cold and wet.
It attacked the branches
And whipped the fences,
Before falling dead on the ground below.

David Chapman (10)
Borough Green Primary School

CHRISTMAS POEM

Through the frosty window,
Is a welcoming sight.
The roaring, blazing fire
Warms the loveable spaniel.
In the distance sweet voices are heard,
Cosy warm carol singers singing tuneful songs.
Whilst the croaky snore from tired Grandad,
Blows the crinkled up newspaper back and forth.
Beside him is a pine table filled with glorious, scrumptious food,
Waiting to be eaten by the energetic children.
Warming up over the sizzling, popping fire,
Stockings getting dangerously warm.
Christmas cards droop down,
To the heavy breathing of the tail wagging spaniel.
As the warm mince pies and fresh, clean water wait for Santa,
A spiky, sharp Christmas tree just decorated.
The fabulous baubles shining in the glittery tree lights,
As the every-sized presents gather round huddling closely
                                            to the rough trunk,
Through the diagonal window lush, cold snow is falling,
A sign that it's Christmas again.

Rebecca Swann (9)
Borough Green Primary School

QUEEN OF THE SKY

A new day starts, the birds are in flight,
Rainbow dances down and makes the sky bright.
She spreads her vibrant dress as she twists and bends
She sprays the world with colours and makes sun and rain friends.

She paints the clouds blue, pink and green
The world admiring her fluorescent sheen.
She leaps to the sky in a beautiful arch
Just like a palace where soldiers march.

She laughs and tosses her multicoloured head,
Ridding the world from all of its dread.
Like a blanket, she wraps up the darkening sky
And stays there to comfort it, till morning is nigh.

Joanna O'Connor (11)
Borough Green Primary School

THE COLOURS OF CHRISTMAS

Christmas is red
Furry red stockings resting above the fire,
Rudolph's nose shimmering in the distance,
The red breast of the robin bobbing up and down,
Tinsel sparkling on cold, blustery nights
And Santa's coat dripping on the soft snow.

Christmas is green
A flash green Christmas tree hanging onto its baubles,
Holly leaves twitching in the hallway,
Crackers waiting patiently in the box,
Mistletoe waiting for something exciting to happen
And twinkling lights shining on the Christmas tree.

Christmas is white
Sparkling snowflakes filling the sky,
Icicles hanging from the rooftops,
Santa's curly beard rustling down the chimney,
Frosty snowmen outside people's doors
And the edges of Santa's coat fidgeting like tinsel.

Christmas is gold
A wishing star shooting across the sky,
Gold, shiny baubles hanging from the Christmas tree,
Gold, shiny wrapping paper
And the angel's halo hovering above her.

Katie Gillard (7)
Borough Green Primary School

THE RIVER

Trickling blue, side to side,
Gently lapping over the cool, quiet rocks,
Swerving in and out of passing waves.
Whispering waves, among each other,
Mustn't wake the grumpy grass.

Slowly, slowly picking up speed,
Waves pretending to not care
To finish first,
But are swimming faster,
Splashing as they go,
When suddenly a wave explodes,
Was a wave, now a scene of bubbles
A scene of bubbles, froth and foam.
Now, because of this mishap of the dark blue wave,
The other waves are tense and are very afraid,
That they might too explode into froth and foam.
But they soon forget all that and start again,
Falling over and somersaulting, trying to win the race.
Then at last it is all over, the clear wave finished first
And celebrates with his friends, in the happy ocean's end.

Daniela Pasquini (11)
Borough Green Primary School

TREES

It looks over the graveyard stones,
Over the dead ones lying there,
It gropes with hands that cling to the dark
The tree then stops with one grimacing stare.

In the sun it smiles and plays with all,
In the golden glow of the pendulum long since swung,
It dances merrily with the breeze,
You see, it is good and kind until the night's begun.

A sinister shadow towers up and reaches to the clouds,
It looks upon a child's face and laughs an evil howl.
It is a crooked figure, a statue in the wind,
An owl then hoots to signal the trees are on the prowl.

Kirstie Keable (10)
Borough Green Primary School

A TROPICAL RAINFOREST

In the still, scarlet sky the warm, gentle sun is going to sleep,
As it touches the swaying, calm trees.

Birds fly to their nests in the canopy layer,
Singing beautiful lullabies.

Across the motionless river you can just catch a glimpse of a sinuous,
                                                    hardworking fisherman
Digging a deep hole to prepare for a warm, cosy fire.

Through the fragile window of an ancient hut on stilts
Sits an exhausted, poor man eating his roast boar.

Children play by the peaceful river
As the dark, shady leaves of gentle swaying palm trees
                dangle into the motionless river.

A hungry, hissing anaconda rapidly wraps itself round an
                                            overhanging branch,
As a concealed, inconspicuous capybara sleeps on a shadowy rock.

A silent, conceited, disdainful stork perches in an unbalanced way
                                                    on one leg,
In this peaceful tropical rainforest.

Sarah Guest (9)
Borough Green Primary School

FIRE

Crackling fire flies across the sky like a jet-black crow,
Constantly flaming everything it sees.
Amber and crimson colours rise from the emerald trees
Using the silent wind as their guide.
It stalks the land from east to west like a blasphemous predator,
The shining parent looks down from above.
It smoulders plants to the ground
Signals death with reeking smoke waves.
Sometimes he has enough of vigorous destroying
And generously helps with tiring household work.
Then tranquilly sets off again,
To alight in a diminutive forest.
Gleefully it rolls around,
But hears a wailing, roaring siren.
It rapidly shoots towards its parents,
They smile at him with rousing glee,
They see bright shining lights,
Then they strike.

Nicholas Burton (9)
Borough Green Primary School

RIVER

Little river learning to run,
Twisting and turning, having fun.
Now comes the brave part -
Making the jump into the big pool below.

Joining friends from long ago,
Saying his hellos,
Racing each other side by side,
To see who can get there first.

Rushing angrily past the rocks,
And fish in their pretty frocks,
Jumping and slurping at the water's edge,
Until he splits up from the rest and departs.

Now he's at the sea,
He can quietly be,
In peace forever,
Apart from the whisper of the waves.

Hannah Cross (11)
Borough Green Primary School

A Mountain Of Fire

The volcano of Sicily has a rumble in its stomach
Tossing its wild head of fire.
He has awoken from deepest slumber
Aroused was he, by mankind
These things have taken over Earth
Which was once a savage place.

Finally opening his mouth
Ready to roar and use destruction,
Mankind is history after this eruption.
Retching lava violently over Mascali
Destroying anything in its fiery path
My mission is accomplished.

Sliding into his white-hot bed
Sleeps a century away.

Russell McEwan (11)
Borough Green Primary School

AN AUTUMN POEM

Dawn grows bigger as the day grows older
Autumn nights are cold in ploughed fields.

In the distance beyond the cottages
Two stubborn grave diggers dig up graves
Whilst a farmer collects the corn in his field.

A poor peasant sits in the stocks
While children throw rotten fruit at him.

The river flows gently as the windmill sails
Do not turn.

This happens on an autumn day.

Kahn Cooper (9)
Borough Green Primary School

HARVEST IN TUDOR TIMES

As the golden sun rises
The black ducking stool waits in the river
The wooden plough starts
Ploughed straw lies on chestnut-coloured ruts.
Whilst the rowdy children play
Birds are collecting, ready to migrate.
A lonely girl plays with her hoop,
The historic windmill twirls gradually,
The cracked cottages stand wordlessly.
The bare trees drop their vibrant leaves
And the gleaming sun shines
On this Tudor day.

Alexandra Saunders (10)
Borough Green Primary School

THE GROWING RIVER

Tributary, tributary
Swaying through the countryside
Silently, silently
Flowing very timidly.

River, river
Pushing against the banks,
Strengthening, strengthening
Its force could make you quiver.

Estuary, estuary
Greeting the sea,
Widening, widening
It's much too wide for me.

Scott Treleaven (10)
Borough Green Primary School

AEROPLANE

The engines roared
And out heat was poured
It sprinted down the runway
And leapt in the air.

The guns spat out bullets
As missiles were launched out of their cages.
It fell out of the air
And jumped back up again.

It ran across the horizon
And swooped towards home
It waited to land
And finally the wheels thumped on the runway.

Thomas Hinkin (10)
Borough Green Primary School

THE WIND

The wild wind,
Fights against the trees,
Trying to knock them over,
While eating away at the leaves.

The wild wind,
Does not succeed,
So it walks away,
To return the next day.

The wild wind,
Tries a different tactic,
And pulls it out of the ground,
But this time he has succeeded.

Ryan Wyatt (10)
Borough Green Primary School

WIND

Whining at the houses,
Eating children's hats,
Fighting with the trees,
Wrestling with the rain.

Sweeping the leaves,
Kicking the bins,
Roaring at the adults,
Pushing them aside.

Calming down,
Spitting out hats,
Dropping the leaves,
Running away.

Florence Bailey (10)
Borough Green Primary School

AFTER CHRISTMAS DINNER

While the turkey and stuffing settles down in their stomachs
The eager children come into the room.
The quiet room.
In the middle of the wall the blazing fire flares,
Eating up all that's in the grate,
Flickering, sparkling as if it were alive.
Beside it lies the lustrous coal scuttle
On the pitch-dark floor.
A sky-scraping, jade Christmas tree planted in a bucket
Stands in front of the delicately decorated window.
Red, yellow sofas sit on guard,
Guarding the white door,
Above the sofa beautifully coloured cards dangle.
The chestnut-coloured wood floor leads up to the velvet rug
On which sits the chocolate-coloured table.
On the table a glass with deep red, damson gin was placed.
Out of the delicately decorated window snow falls,
Building up a layer as it goes.
Carol singers sing merrily and joyfully.
Shh! There in a creaky rocking chair, Grandad is asleep.
The excited children giggle on hearing his whistling snore!
On his head, just over his eye, a red and green party hat is perched.
As the children edge closer their eyes enlarge,
Seeing the presents stacked under the Christmas tree
The wrapping paper bright blue, the brightest blue ever,
With little yellow stars.
All are stacked under the Christmas tree waiting to be opened on
Christmas Day.

Bob Entwistle (9)
Borough Green Primary School

FIRE

F laming and spitting,
I t twists and turns
R olling and tumbling,
E mbers are burned.

F laring its nostrils
I t shakes its head
R ipples around the room
E mbers lay dead.

F ighting a battle of life and death
I t gives an almighty sigh
R uns out of breath
E ventually dies.

Catriona Rowbury (10)
Borough Green Primary School

THE DOOR

Go and open the creaky door,
The chocolate man might be there.

Go and open the enchanted door,
You might see a big grisly bear.

Go and open the steel door,
Our Chinese might have arrived.

Go and open the double-glazed door,
Your dad may be home.

Go and open the unlocked door,
Miss Leeson might be there.

Jamie Cutts (8)
Cage Green Primary School

IF I LEFT MY TOWN I WOULD MISS . . .

If I left my town . . .
I'd miss all my best friends
And my neighbours next door.

I'd miss my school very much
And the teachers I like a lot.

I'd miss the house I grew up in
And going to the town.

I'd miss the shops that had sweets in
And the park which I played in.

I'd remember when I fell off the bench and cut my knee
And the special day I got a cat called Dougal.

That's what I would miss,
That's what I would miss
And remember.

Amy Pyne (9)
Cage Green Primary School

THE DOOR

Go and open the door
There might be a cartoon character.

Go and open the door
The wonderful Tom and Jerry might be there.

Go and open the door
There may be a dangerous Pikachu waiting to thunder.

Anna-Marie Buckley (8)
Cage Green Primary School

THE AMAZING TENNIS POEM

I go to the tennis courts at the LTA
There I enrolled and learnt how to play.
We play mini tennis, Red, Orange and Green,
You can stay and play Bronze, Silver and Gold if you're keen.
All Henman's start somewhere and this is the place,
So if you're interested tell Linda and cut to the chase.

Ian's the boss, he is coach number one,
And he thinks he has us under his thumb.
We play along and do as we're told,
And as a result our game's getting bold.
He shows me how to make my racket swing,
And insists that I always get my serve in.

Pete is next - coach number two,
He's taught me everything that I've learnt to do.
He serves a serve all dressed in white,
That travels the court at the speed of light.
He teaches us the moves, back hand and lob,
He teaches us nutrition, crisps, chocolate and pop.

Last but not least is Adam - coach number three,
He mainly teaches Reds, which fills him with glee.
He'll teach you the basics when you first start,
Holding the racket is quite a fine art.
Soon you'll be hitting the ball through the air,
But be careful it doesn't touch Adam's gelled hair.

Now I'm in Green, I'm down at the base,
Trying to serve a big smashing ace.
I need to practice my serve and volley,
It seems to behave like a Sainsbury's trolley.
I try really hard - about that there's no doubt,
I'm just waiting for people to stop calling 'O*ut!*'

I've been keeping fit and making new friends,
Wimbledon is where I hope this all ends.
Playing tennis is really great fun,
I recommend it to everyone.
Now I've written this poem, there's only one catch,
It really is time for me to call 'Game, set and match.'

Matthew Derrick (9)
Cage Green Primary School

WITCH'S SPELL

Double, double, toil and trouble,
Fire burn and cauldron bubble!

Mushy brains and nose of dog,
Eye of eel and tongue of frog!

Double, double, toil and trouble,
Fire burn and cauldron bubble!

Mucky children's scabby knees,
And blood-filled, thirsty, cats' fleas!

Double, double, toil and trouble,
Fire burn and cauldron bubble!

Spirit's toenails gone mouldy,
Corpse's throat that's quite bloody!

Double, double, toil and trouble,
Fire burn and cauldron bubble!

Elephant's trunk and a soul,
Ear of bear from the North Pole!

Double, double, toil and trouble,
Fire burn and cauldron bubble!

Grace Dugdale (11)
Cage Green Primary School

THE DOOR

Go and open the door,
Maybe a bloodthirsty dog's sitting on the doorstep
Or a big-headed giant.

Go and open the door,
Maybe beautiful Snow White's waiting for a cup of tea
Or ice cream's hovering above the door.

Go and open the door,
Maybe a snapping crocodile is sleeping
Or there's an army of soldiers.

Go and open the door,
Maybe there's a creamy chocolate factory or
Miss Leeson or your best friends.
Even if there's a wolf there
At least there'll be something.

Laura Pullen (8)
Cage Green Primary School

THE DOOR

Go and open the door,
Maybe there is a magic waterfall, rippling over the edge.

Go and open the door,
Maybe my best friend is waiting for me.

Go and open the door,
Maybe a cheetah is waiting to swiftly pounce on me.

Go and open the door,
Maybe a brutal witch is waiting to seize me
And you won't want to meet her on a dark, gloomy, eerie night.

Tonya Streeter (8)
Cage Green Primary School

THE DOOR

Go and open the door
There might be a creepy, crawly spider.

Go and open the door,
There could be a colourful, sparkling rainbow.

Go and open the door,
There could be a lion just waiting to leap up on you.

Go and open the door,
There might be a beaming sunshine.

Go and open the door,
There could be Jesus floating on a gleaming white cloud.

Go and open the door there may be a lot.

Emma Saunders (8)
Cage Green Primary School

THE DOOR

Go and open the door,
Maybe there will be a ghost town or a graveyard.

Go and open the door,
Maybe there will be a massive pixie garden or a big waterfall.

Go and open the door,
Maybe there is a red-hot devil.

Go and open the door,
Even if you see nothing.

Go and open the door,
At least you will know what's there!

Annabel Marriott (9)
Cage Green Primary School

THE HOUSE I'LL NEVER FORGET

When I left my house
I missed the shadows in the garden
And the bright orange poppies growing here and there.

I missed the windows that wouldn't stay open
And the cellar that was wet and damp.

I missed the front garden with a great, big conker tree
And the hall with narrow stairs.

I missed the bedroom with a slanted roof
And the bedrooms with wooden floors.

I remembered the day our house got struck by lightning
And the day I fell down the stairs!

Sophie Thompson (10)
Cage Green Primary School

THE DOOR

Go and open the door,
There might be a white and grey wolf howling at the moon.

Go and open the door,
There might be a pale white ghost floating towards *you!*

Go and open the door,
There might be a bar of creamy brown chocolate
                                      sitting on your deckchair.

Go and close the door,
It's too cold and frosty, brrrr!

Tarn McGibbon (8)
Cage Green Primary School

THE DOOR

Go and open the door,
There might be a plain old garden
Or my kind English teacher Miss Leeson.

Go and open the door,
Maybe there will be a garden full of scrumptious, hot, fudge chocolate.

Go and open the door,
There could be a magic theme park.

Go and open the door,
There might be a kind Mrs Miller.

Go and open the door,
At least there will be a touch of wind.

Ellisha Owen (8)
Cage Green Primary School

THE DOOR

Go and open the door,
Maybe outside there is a spooky, old ghost
And the ghost's dog.

Go and open the door,
Maybe outside there is a gruesome, old teacher
Or maybe a disco.

Go and open the door,
Maybe outside there is a fox's eyeball
Or maybe a brush.

Go and open the door,
Maybe outside there is a flock of sheep
Or maybe a sheepdog.

Sophie Littlechild (8)
Cage Green Primary School

IF I LEFT MY HOUSE I'D MISS . . .

If I left my house I'd miss . . .
The first day I met my favourite neighbour called Ken
And the sound of the owl tweeting every night.

I'd miss my neighbours knocking on my door,
And the day when I lost my favourite Beanie called Bananas.

I'd miss seeing the monkeys on our TV
And the elephants and the giraffes making really loud sounds.

I'd miss my brother singing his best songs,
And I'd miss my mum dancing while she does her ironing.

I'd miss cuddling my cats who where really furry,
And when I kept on falling down the stairs when I was a young girl.

I wouldn't miss my brother bullying me all the time,
And when he annoyed me all the time as well.

I'd remember the day I tripped up my bike and nearly broke my arm
And the day when there was a big spider walking
                              across our front room floor.

That's what I'd miss and remember if I left my house!

Rebecca Eldridge (10)
Cage Green Primary School

MY POEM

If I left my school . . .
I'd miss the times when I slid down the banister,
And the smell of school dinners.

I'd miss all the times when I got first places in sports day,
And the things that I have won in competitions.

I'd miss all the times when I lost things in bets,
And playing football for the school team.

I'd remember when an acorn fell on my head and I had a bump,
And when I got two stars on my homework.

Sam Wesley (10)
Cage Green Primary School

THINGS TO REMEMBER ABOUT MY HOUSE

If I left my house . . .
I'd miss the squeaking swing in the back garden
And the creaking landing floor.

I'd miss the dripping kitchen tap
And the leaky draining board.

I'd miss the smooth velvety feel of my bedroom walls
And the smell that fills our living room.

I'd miss the hatch that goes from our kitchen to dining room
And the sloping roof on the front of our house.

I'd miss the big conifer trees in the back garden
And the sliding door.

I'd remember the day I crashed into a dustbin on my bike
And nearly broke my arm
And the sad day my rabbit had to be put down.

I'd remember the day I almost fell out the window
And the day I nearly dropped my dinner on the floor.

I'd remember the day a spider crawled up my leg
And the night I rolled out of bed.

Stephanie Bradley (10)
Cage Green Primary School

WHAT I WILL MISS WHEN I MOVE HOUSE

If I left my house . . .
I'd miss my pond in the backyard,
And I'd also miss the loud patting sound on my sunroom's roof.

I'd miss the sound of the floorboard creaking as I came in the room,
And the sour smell of my bathroom.

I'd remember the feel of the wood when I opened the wardrobe.
And I'd remember the look of our shiny bath.

But I definitely wouldn't forget my friends that I played with.

Nicholas Carlton (10)
Cage Green Primary School

IF I LEFT MY HOUSE

If I left my house I'd miss the radiator that made a noise at night
And I'd miss the smell of the forest that connects to my back garden.

I'd miss the frogs that jump out of the pond in the forest
And I'd miss the time when I dropped my china doll on the floor
                                                  and broke it.

I'd remember the time when I drank a bottle of Fanta with a fly in it.

Franki Gower (9)
Cage Green Primary School

MOVING HOUSE

When I move house . . .
I'll miss my lucky 1p that I lost beneath our carpet,
And the hole my dog dug in the backyard.

I'll miss the Blu-Tac on the wall where my posters hung,
And the scratches on the kitchen door my dog made.

I'll miss the red crayon face I made on my pink bedroom wall,
And the place where my King Charles spaniel died.

I'll remember the day I had my bedroom decorated,
And on my eighth birthday party when I fell in the paddling pool.

Nicola Wood (9)
Cage Green Primary School

IF I LEFT MY HOUSE . . .

If I left my house . . .
I'd miss the way my airing cupboard used to click.

And I would miss when the shower curtain fell down
When we had a shower.

I'd miss the smell from the guinea pigs in the garden
And opening my window and looking out at the next-door's garden.

I'd remember when I broke my bed when I was seven
And the wonderful smell of my room.

Jess Owen (10)
Cage Green Primary School

MY HOUSE

I'd miss my tree that I named Ian Wright,
And my guinea pig's grave that I buried in the night.

I'd miss the smell of my dad's compost heap,
And the bumps in the night that make me have a fright.

I'd miss my swing that I swing on every day,
And my lovely big garden where I love to play.

Alice Plummer (10)
Cage Green Primary School

IF I LEFT THE AIR FORCE

If I left the Air Force
I'd miss doing a somersault in the air
And flying into the water on practice, flying a MiG-16.
I'd also miss beating the enemy at war
And I'd miss touching the control stick to fire the torpedoes.
I'd miss the boss shouting at me if I had failed something
And Private Sally kissing me when I won the war
                              against the enemy's army, by myself.
I remember the day I became a private,
And when I was promoted to boss!

Stuart Obbard (10)
Cage Green Primary School

IF I LEFT MY HOUSE . . .

If I left my house . . .
I'd miss my garden and the way the grass shone in the sun.

I'd miss my room that was always warm in winter
And my thick blue carpet.

I'll always remember going to Monkey World
And coming home to my warm and cosy bed.

Jamie Bott (9)
Cage Green Primary School

WHAT I'D MISS AT HOME

I'd miss my animal graveyard under the back tree
And the special badge that got lost under the floorboard.

I'd miss the trees I climb through
And when I like going behind the shed.

I'd miss the way the school is really close
And the way I tripped on the top step.

I will remember my ninth birthday
And last Christmas when I threw up at the dentists before going home.

Emma Gray (10)
Cage Green Primary School

THE DOOR

Go and open the door,
I think there are some prowling dogs out there.

Go and open the door,
Maybe there is a stampede of elephants.

Go and open the door,
For your teacher has her hands full.

Go and open the door,
For your friend is waiting for you.

James Burton (8)
Cage Green Primary School

IF I LEFT MY HOUSE . . .

If I left my house . . .
I'd miss my red hat
That I lost and never found
And the frogs in the back garden that hopped on my feet.
I'd miss the fireplace that kept me warm in the winter
And the playroom where I play on the computer and play with my toys.

Hayley Francis (9)
Cage Green Primary School

THE DOOR

Go and open the door,
Maybe there's a jet plane bombing
Or a cute cat.

Go and open the door,
Maybe a chainsaw is cutting a tree
Or you'll see a slimy alien.

Go and open the door,
Maybe a rotten skeleton is there.

Go and open the door,
Maybe there's a dead zombie
Or a boiling explosion.

Don't open the door!

Matthew Evans (9)
Cage Green Primary School

THE DOOR

Go and open the door,
Maybe there's a beautiful unicorn
Or a grizzly bear.

Go and open the door,
Maybe there is loads of delicious chocolate
Or a sack of ice cream.

Go and open the door,
Maybe there's a gruesome vampire
Or a pot of ice cream.

Go and shut the door!

Naomi Glazier (9)
Cage Green Primary School

IF I LEFT SCHOOL . . .

If I left my school . . .
I'd miss the girls toilets where I hang out
And my chatty best friend Naomi.

I'd miss the teachers shouting at me
And the naughty bullies.

I'd miss the books that I got ideas from,
And the book weeks when a writer came in.

I'd miss the good old years,
And the bad years.

I'd miss the lunch room where I ate
And the huts where I learnt.

I wouldn't miss any of the horrible teachers.

Vicky Cole (10)
Cage Green Primary School

THE DOOR

Go and open the door,
Maybe there is a wizened face.

Go and open the door,
Maybe there is an extraordinary present.

Go and open the door,
Maybe there is a neglected house
Or an eerie graveyard!

Don't open the door
Because there is a bloodthirsty hound!

Josef Hills (9)
Cage Green Primary School

IF I LEFT MY HOUSE . . .

If I left my house . . .
I'd miss the crack in my bedroom ceiling,
And my fish's grave in the back garden.
I'd miss the button I lost in the washing machine,
And my bedroom with the creaky floorboards.
I'd miss the squirrels that live in our chimney,
And the three inch dolly that I found under our carpet.

I'd remember the day I nearly fell out of my window
And when I fell out of my top bunk.
I'd remember the day a big spider crawled up my leg,
And when I fell down the stairs and sprained my ankle.
I'd remember the window smashing,
And the glass shattering into tiny little pieces.

Robyn Morris (10)
Cage Green Primary School

IF I LEFT MY RIDING CLUB

If I left my riding club
I'd miss riding out in the rain.
And the way Rodney sucked his door
I'd miss jumping jumps.

And miss the smell of fresh hay
I'd miss the feel when Madam was brushed.

And when Polly went mad
I'd miss walking out in the mud to catch the horses
And when I won fourth place in dressage riding Nickel.

I'd remember when I first went riding
And when I almost fell off Blackie.

Kristy Dugdale (9)
Cage Green Primary School

IF I LEFT MY HOUSE . . .

If I left my house . . .
I'd miss the squirrels that climbed up and down our oak tree
And the birds that sang in the morning.

I'd miss the sheep in the field
And the tractor that drove along the grass.

I'd miss the strawberry bush on the rockery
And the tomato plants.

I'd remember the time there was a spider on our bathroom ceiling
And we called him Sid
And the foxes that kept me awake at night.

Charlotte Coulter (10)
Cage Green Primary School

THE DOOR

Go and open the door, maybe there are
    Some framed photos of your grandparents.
Go and open the door, maybe there are
    ' Ferocious wolves dashing to crunch you up.
Go and open the door, maybe there is
    A fluffy cat waiting for you to stroke it.
Go and open the door, maybe there are
    Some spooky noises that are really scary.
Go and open the door, maybe there's
    A white horse waiting calmly.
Go and open the door, maybe there's
    A dinosaur waiting to crack your bones.

Do you want me
    To open the door?

Jamie Matheson (8)
Cage Green Primary School

THE DOOR

Go and open the door,
There might be a beautiful dove.
Go and open the door,
There might be a sweet-smelling flower.
Go and open the door,
My best friend might be waiting.

Go and open the door,
There might be some spectacular fireworks.
Go and open the door,
There might be some delicious chocolates,
Go and open the door,
My best friend might be waiting.

Go and open the door,
There might be a marvellous magician.
Go and open the door,
There might be a delicate fairy.
Don't open the door
My best friend isn't there.

Lauren Goad (9)
Cage Green Primary School

THE NIGHT I LOST MY CAT

I miss her black and white fur
And her warm, soft touch.
I miss her purr in the morning
And her miaowing at night.
But the thing I won't forget
Is that she was mine.

Amber Page (9)
Cage Green Primary School

THE DOOR

Go and open the door,
Maybe there's a waggling tail!
Go and open the door,
Maybe there's a piece of frail silk!
Go and open the door,
Maybe there's a burglar trying to bail!
Go and open the door,
Maybe there's the Holy Grail!

Go and open the door,
Maybe there's a bloodthirsty bat!
Go and open the door,
Maybe there's a mountain troll!
Go and open the door,
Maybe there's a sewage rat!
Go and open the door,
Maybe there's a chicken roll!

Go and open the door,
Maybe your fate has come!

Jack Powell (8)
Cage Green Primary School

SANTA

He is big and bold and quite old
He is fat and round
At night he doesn't make a sound.
He is dressed in red and comes when we're in bed
His boots are black and he has toys in his sack
His sleigh is pulled by reindeer, across the sky so clear.

Martyn Pyne (10)
Cage Green Primary School

THE DOOR

Go and open the door
Maybe there's sneaky Mrs Miller
Or fantastic Miss Leeson,
Even a haunted, spooky house.

Go and open the door,
Maybe there's a cheerful Santa
Or a bloodthirsty vampire.

Go and open the door,
Maybe there's a pale white unicorn
Or a sack of precious money,
Even a grizzly lion.

Go and open the door,
Maybe there are scary ghosts,
Even a young, sweet baby.

Abby Jeffery (8)
Cage Green Primary School

IF I LEFT MY HOUSE . . .

If I left my house . . .
I'd miss the fluffy squirrel burying acorns in the back garden,
And the big, fat toad that lives in our pond.

I'd miss the sound of steps moving across the lounge,
And the tapping under the floorboards.

I'd miss the little door mice running in the back garden,
And the mouse that bit me and never let go.

I'd remember the time my cat died, just before my birthday,
And the time I shook the lights downstairs when I popped!

Hayley Eldridge
Cage Green Primary School

THE DOOR

Go and open the door,
There might be a green garden
Or a kissing tree
Or a ghost peeping
Up on you.

Go and open the door,
As something is there.

Go and open the door,
Before Jamie Cutts will come and . . . eat you.

Go and open the door,
There might be a green garden
Or a kissing tree
Or a ghost peeping
Up on you.

Brogan Hook (8)
Cage Green Primary School

LEOPARD

The glamorous figure moves through the glistening grass;
The deer, the prey, is unaware he's there,
Delicately drinking beside the river bed,
Ready to run should danger raise its head.
The leopard, waiting as still as a statue
Waits, then springs through the air,
Like an acrobat on a trapeze,
The deer senses danger,
He flees and is gone, like a leaf in the breeze.

Emma Kirkpatrick (10)
Cage Green Primary School

THE DOOR

Go and open the door,
Maybe there is a devil or a nice, old teacher.

Go and open the door,
Maybe there is a tornado or your head teacher.

Go and open the door,
Maybe there is Scooby Doo or a magic parade.

Go and open the door,
Maybe there is a Tyrannosaurus-rex or your gang.

Go and open the door,
Maybe there is a gang of lions.

Go and open the door,
Maybe your best friend is waiting to see you.

So go and open the door,
The mystery . . .
Awaits.

Joshua Moor (9)
Cage Green Primary School

HIDDEN TREASURES

Hidden treasures here and there
Even everywhere
Some in the sea
In the coral reef

They could be you
To your parents
But mostly in the sea
And you might be the hidden key!

Under the sea where fish live
They protect the treasure
Under the sea
All of it just for me

I will share some to the poor
None of it to be rich
Some of it hidden in the seaweed
I will help those only in need.

Jack Everitt (9)
Clare House Primary School

THE JUMPER

I run and run
Through the thick fiery sun.
Now I'm going to jump over the line
Yes! I hope the trophy's mine.
The next round,
People are cheering in the crowd.
Jump man, jump man,
I know you can.
Jump and fly,
Through the sky.
Bounce man, bounce,
Like a cat ready to pounce.
I hope I'm not last,
Just because I'm not fast.
But I know I'm going to jump over the van,
I know I can, I really can.
I'm just in time,
Yes! The trophy's mine.

Olivia Holmes (9)
Clare House Primary School

MY CARNIVAL POEM

Everybody is dancing and having lots of fun,
People sharing happy feelings everywhere around me,
People are celebrating under the sun,
Come on, the music is starting.

Everybody will dance tonight,
Swirling colours of green and red.
Soon the clock will strike midnight,
But everyone shall carry on.

People are dressing up as cats,
Or even a mermaid with long hair
And sometimes even bats,
Oh no, it's time to go home.

Madalen Weeks (8)
Clare House Primary School

CARNIVAL COSTUMES

Some costumes are bright,
Some costumes are beautiful,
Some costumes are worn at night
And some costumes are colourful.

All costumes are beautiful things
Some of them have wonderful wings,
Some of them are to do with kings
And at least one person in their costume sings.

All costumes are as colourful as can be,
Some costumes stand out in the dark,
All costumes are brighter than me
And some costumes set off a spark.

James Jarratt (9)
Clare House Primary School

THE CARNIVAL IS COMING

The carnival is coming
We're terribly excited
Have some fun one and all
The carnival is coming.

Swirling colours of purple and blues
Beautiful dancers rushing by
Goodness me what lovely shoes
The carnival is coming.

Oh no Mum's still making cakes and sweets
They smell so delicious, hurry quick
Look at that dress it's like lovely white sheets
The carnival is here.

Hannah Caswall (8)
Clare House Primary School

CARNIVAL POEM

Colourful dresses and shimmering gowns,
Huge feather hats,
The carnival is in town,
The parade has begun.

A girl on the float,
Is smiling and dancing,
Wearing a shiny, sparkling coat,
As the music plays happily.

It's all so beautiful and bright,
Like a line of
Dancing street lights,
I love the carnival.

Hannah Jaroudy (8)
Clare House Primary School

THE SHINING SUN

The sun is rising,
The clouds are breaking,
The puddles are vanishing,
Keep waiting for the sun.

The sky is getting lighter,
The world is getting warmer,
The people start getting excited,
Keep waiting for the sun.

The sky starts losing its clouds,
The moon has gone away,
The animals are very happy,
The shining sun.

Harriet Dempsey (9)
Clare House Primary School

OCTOPUS

He lurks beneath the sea,
And never sees the light,
He is the one that scares you,
In the middle of the night.

He knows you are always there,
But never sees your face,
For he lies deep in the ocean,
Hating all the human race.

Every second you are breathing,
And every time you speak,
Octopus is sleeping,
Among the coral reef.

Yasmin Hatfield (8)
Clare House Primary School

HIDDEN TREASURES

Hidden treasures under the sea
Just waiting to be found by me.
Hidden treasures under the sea
Just wonder if there's a golden key.

Hidden treasures underground
Just waiting to be found.
Hidden treasures under ground
Just wait for a silver pound.

Hidden treasures all around
The glittering, sparkling sound.
Hidden treasures all around
Just wonder if they will be found.

Sam Smith (9)
Clare House Primary School

MY CAT JASPER

When my cat Jasper first wakes up
He usually has a drink from a nice round cup.
Jasper has his breakfast biscuits or meat
And he even sometimes has a treat.
He goes out the window every day
Because he wants to go out and play.
He plays with Birtie the dog
And they both like to jump on a log.
Jasper seems a sweet cat
But he's mine and that's that.

Hannah Page (9)
Downe Primary School

I AM ...

I am Michael, I like to draw
Things I've seen and things I saw.
I'm a water baby, I love to swim
Hanging out with my mates is never dim.
I like sport, rugby and tennis
Some people say I'm a right little menace.
I love to run about and play
And watch TV every day.
I love sweets and chocolate too
When you're with me there's lots to do.
I'm the best, I'm never late,
But if I am, I'm worth the wait.
With me you're sure to have some fun
I get on fine with everyone.
I'm very brainy and modest too.
Showing off, I never do.
I am popular, everyone loves me
A smug little know-it-all, I'll never be.

Michael Lever (10)
Downe Primary School

WHAT IS A ... GHOST?

A ghost is its own memory,
Existing in its own world,
A spirit wandering desperately from door to door
What is it looking for?

An indistinct shape,
White and pale,
A shadow, a movement under your bed,
Whispering, whispering,
Can it really be dead?

So look out, he's coming to haunt you,
A deadly, sinister creature,
Forever watching, forever seeing,
Wanting, wanting,
Contact with a human being.

Danielle Leonard (9)
Downe Primary School

AUTUMN COLOURS

Colours scattered everywhere
Up and down and through the air.
Trees with hair
Are going bald,
Nature's sleeping,
The breeze is cold.

Colours scattered everywhere
Up and down and through the air.
The light turns off,
Colours fade
Leaves in heaps,
Children wade.

Colours scattered everywhere
Up and down and through the air.
Polished conkers
In green shells,
Each colour has a meaning,
A story to tell.

Adam Young (10)
Downe Primary School

WHAT IS A GHOST?

A ghost is a sheet as white as a bone.
A ghost is a fright when you are all alone.
A ghost is a scare when nobody is there.
A ghost is a thing with a pale white glare.
A ghost is a spirit that is no longer alive.
A ghost is a thing with its own little hive.
A ghost is a thing that cannot sing.
A ghost is a thing that can't stop wailing.
A ghost is a shiver under your bed.
A ghost is a thing that can chop off your head!

Erin Gilbrook (10)
Downe Primary School

WHAT IS A . . . GHOST?

A ghost is an image under your bed,
The sound of the dead repeating in your head.
A no longer living memory,
Waiting for its bicentenary.
Moaning and groaning in castles and homes,
A ghost is a guardian of those who are alone.

Jack Jeffrey (9)
Downe Primary School

AUTUMN

Bright colours faded away
Replaced by browns, gold, orange and grey.
Gradually the leaves die and tumble down
All those beautiful leaves now lay on the ground

Children kick the leaves about
Others just jump and shout!
Many kids make leaf bases,
See the look on their faces.

Samuel Davey (10)
Downe Primary School

AUTUMN COLOURS

Autumn is a rampaging tiger in the woods,
Autumn is a kid playing in the leaves.
But best of all are the colours,
Red, green, whispery gold,
Crimson, brown, bronze and
Chestnut-coloured copper.
But when the winter comes,
And the sun goes down,
Autumn is an old man that has lived his life.

Charlie Matthews (11)
Downe Primary School

LABRADOR

Honey-eyed, brown velvet, shovel head
He's king of the castle on Mum and Dad's bed.
Sunday walks as relaxing as a bomb disposal
As crazy and scatty as a tiger cub pouncing on a spider
Do we cut the blue wire or red?
Loose-wired, hair-triggered, hair-brained
Shovel head.

Sam Garwood (10)
Downe Primary School

A RECIPE FOR A NICER WORLD

Take a slice of friendship,
Add a pinch of trees.
Take a litre of beauty
Including the fresh breeze.

Hope, joy, love let be,
Make everyone become happy.

Take a spoonful of consideration,
To help out all the nation.
Add some kindness to this cake,
Then it's nearly ready to bake.

Hope, joy, love let be,
Make everyone become happy.

Take the sunshine from the sky,
Let everyone learn to fly.
Stop sinful people by the dozen
Now this cake can go in the oven.

Hope, joy, love let be,
Make everyone become happy.

Ryan Sadler (10)
Downe Primary School

WHAT IS A . . . GHOST?

A ghost is a creaky floorboard, waiting in the night,
Spirit behind the curtain, waiting for a fright,
The dustbins clank, who would pull such a prank?
These are the only clues, of which we know what they do.

Jack Jewell (9)
Downe Primary School

BUSTER

My dog likes meats and he likes treats,
But what he likes most is eating the post,
He sits and waits at the door
And picks up letters off the floor.
It is a naughty game but we love him just the same.

Karla Sikora (10)
Downe Primary School

HIDDEN TREASURES

I go to my dad's as happy as can be
Then grandad came up and told me
Of all the weird and strangest things
He told me that they adopted him!

'Adopted who, when and how
I'm going to scream if you don't tell me now!'
'We adopted your dad quite long ago
Oh I'm sorry, didn't you know?'

'Of course I didn't, how can it be,
Why didn't my dad just tell me?'
'Maybe he didn't want to upset you.'
'I would have been happier if I knew!'

I need my dad to shout at soon,
Time's getting on, it's nearly noon,
I've found a secret
It's good and bad.

But I want to find out about
My real nan and grandad!

Robyn Willard (11)
Hildenborough CE Primary School

HIDDEN TREASURE

I was playing with my toys
When two things came in. Oh yeah! They're my parents
Both came in, I was trying to play.
They're talking gibberish, goo, goo, gah, gah,
They're talking like they're from another planet.

Then they picked me up,
I was the best boy in the world.
They were about to say something good, in a patronising way
'You're going to have a baby brother.'
Next thing they knew they had problems,
My tantrum went on for hours,
By this time my parents were having a breakdown
They were worse than me.

Mum was getting fat.
Too much second helpings!
Next thing we knew . . .
Ahhh, the house nearly fell down!

Dad had his car out before you could say goo, goo, gah, gah,
He went speeding down the road, then remembered Mum.
He shoved her in the car and was off.

They came back. There was a surprise for me.
It was a baby, how sweet he was,
He looked worse than Dad, nevertheless, he's lovely.
He's a real treasure.
All this and I'm only three!

Hamish De Rusett (11)
Hildenborough CE Primary School

HIDDEN TREASURE

Out in the zones of World War II
In 2002,
I was walking
When I tripped on something hard and metallic.
Now what is this? I thought to myself,
A big rock with squares on it?
It was a grenade,
A grenade it was, just lying there in my hand,
No peg and all
Just sitting there in my hand.
'Holy Mackerel!' I said out loud
'I'm gonna die, it's a bloomin' grenade!'
I threw it down and ran,
Ran and ran and ran.
Hang on a minute, I thought to myself,
That grenade hasn't exploded for all these sixty years!
But I still ran, just in case.
I reached the nearest tree and looked back
Oh well, I'll go back over, it hasn't blown up.
When I reached it I picked it up,
Then ran home with it to my room.
The next day I came out to search for
More hidden treasures
And what did I find . . .
A bullet.
A very small bullet
'Cor, I'll bet that's a 7.9mm!' I exclaimed
I was pleased, oh I was pleased!
Grenade and bullet,
What a find!

Patrick Duckworth (10)
Hildenborough CE Primary School

HIDDEN TREASURE

A golden beam of sunlight pierced the beach
The azure waves licked the sand
Like the fruit of Earth,
God held Heaven in his hand.
The sky of light blue icing
That stretched there day and night
That iced the cake of nature
Sprinkled with clouds of pearly white.
Waves rocking like a cradle
Fishes swimming in a dream
Pearls are a treasure of the sea
The pinks, the whites and cream.
But the sun, it clouded over
The waves turned murky grey
The golden fruit turned mouldy
It was like Hell, you might say.
All it took was a sweep of wind,
The waves became rolling stones,
They swept me up and took me down,
All I could hear were sighs and groans.
I thought of the future
But it clouded up my mind
Darkness loomed in front
Death closed in behind.
But someone grabbed my hand
And turned the darkness into light,
They are the real hidden treasures,
They keep well out of sight.

Katy Richardson (11)
Hildenborough CE Primary School

HIDDEN TREASURES

As I walk through my secret forest
Time ticks by with graceful ease,
Birds and bees whizz round my head
And flutter on the breeze.

Where is the middle of this forest?
Trees whisper and giggle in the wind,
And lift up people's spirits
As they have been doing for a million years!

Leaves grow then slowly fall to the ground
And scatter all around
Twenty trees bend over and try to kiss the earth
And twenty trees stand tall and touch the sky.

Great eagles fly above me
And badgers dig below me
And the flowers grow beside me
And beauty's everywhere.

Amy Cowlard (11)
Hildenborough CE Primary School

HIDDEN TREASURES

I walked towards the beautiful waterfall
I managed to walk right through it
Came out the other side and found myself
At the entrance of the night sky.
It shone and glittered in my eyes
The moon shines bright like it's on fire
And a flying saucer passes by.

Phoebe Cattley (10)
Hildenborough CE Primary School

HIDDEN TREASURES

A tear that fills a thousand swimming pools.
A laugh that echoes throughout the desert.
A gaze that looks through all eternity.
A smile that lights up our lives
Or a wink of the evil eye.
A cough that shakes the steadiest land.
A cry that kills a million ants.
A questioned face that confuses scientists.
A sneaky voice that annoys teachers.
The last gasp of a bad situation.
A sigh of relief that calms the panicked.
A sneeze that poisons the world.
A squeak as loud as a bomb.
A blink as fast as a wren.
You can't measure
My hidden treasure.

James Denman (10)
Hildenborough CE Primary School

HIDDEN TREASURE

I wish . . .
I wish I could fly as long as I like,
And ride a million miles on my bike.
I wish I could run faster than a cheetah,
And jump like a kangaroo more than a metre.
I wish I could swim as fast as a shark,
And bark louder than a dog can bark.
I wish I could always run in the rain,
And be the driver on a really fast train.

I wish I was on a beach in the sun,
And when I'm there drink loads of rum.
I wish I could catch fish,
So I can have them on my afternoon dish.
It's all just total pleasure,
All that is my hidden treasure.

Richard Hughes (10)
Hildenborough CE Primary School

HIDDEN TREASURES

My best friend's like a treasure to me
He is always there for me.
But then one day he was gone, vanished in a flash of light,
Disappeared into the open world.
How I miss him dearly, I can't think at all,
I have no money to spend,
No friend!
All I have is God to guide me,
I have no family to love.
I lay in bed dreaming for the day
When we will meet again.
Then one day I see a man wounded badly,
He said he was attacked in the dark, dark night!
So I asked his name,
He replied quietly.
It hits me, it was my old friend, he's back - joy!
It was the best day of my life
And from that day on I was rich, rich, rich
And I had my friend back!
He's back to stand by me,
He was a hidden treasure,
Until now!

Mark Pratt (10)
Hildenborough CE Primary School

HIDDEN TREASURES

H ere lies the coral
I t's white like a fluffy cloud
D own beneath the ocean
D olphins dive
E ndless shoals of fish fly by
N ever have I seen such a sight.

T he turtles glide by
R ays riding the waves,
E verything so beautiful
A ngler fish after other fish
S and flying up behind the escaping fish
U nderneath the waterline
R eefs full of wonderful fish
E ndless treasures hidden under the sea.

Leo Hall (10)
Hildenborough CE Primary School

HIDDEN TREASURES

Underneath the clear, rippling water lies an old chest,
A once golden lock and key sticks like a barnacle to the chest,
Surrounded by a cluster of shivering seaweed and guarded by
                                                        a colossal octopus.
Erupting from the chest flows a shoal of tropical fish,
Bright, dazzling colours, shiny, glittery scales dashing like
                                         darts through the underworld.
They became a glimpse of a golden hope,
Sparks of light for life under the sea.

Jessica Gibbs (10)
Hildenborough CE Primary School

SPECIAL

Like leaves on a swaying tree,
Like feathers on a bird,
Like icing on a sponge cake,
Like a silver star streaming across the midnight sky.
Golden sand on a dusty beach
Like wheels on a rusty car,
Pollen in a purple flower.

Like snow on a mountain tip,
Like ink in a pen,
Like sugar on an almond,
Like the hard shell on a turtle's back.

It finishes your life with glee,
To have a special friend!

Naomi Whittome (10)
Hildenborough CE Primary School

TREASURE

A gleaming treasure,
Surrounded by rocks.
A shining light,
At the end of the tunnel,
Possessed by some,
Wanted by all.
Everyone can find their own
But maybe held back by others.
Poor who have it are,
Better off than rich who don't
For money cannot buy it . . .

Freedom!

Andrew Taylor (10)
Hildenborough CE Primary School

HIDDEN TREASURES

'My dad's been to Jupiter.'
   'Well, my dad's been to Mars!'
'My dad's got a new sports car.'
   'Well, my dad's got ten cars!'
'My dad won the lottery.'
   'Well, my dad's a millionaire!'
'My dad's met President Bush.'
   'Well, my dad's met Tony Blair!'
'My dad's swum with dolphins.'
   'Well, my dad's swum with sharks!'
'My dad's got a golden eagle.'
   'Well, my dad's got ten larks!'
'My dad's taking me to Turkey.'
   'Well, my dad's taking me to Devon!'
'My dad's taking me to Spain.'
   'Well, my dad's up in Heaven!'
The group of girls turned round to see,
A pale-faced boy who looked about three.
He turned on his heel and walked away
Then the bell rang out which ended play.
And from then on, they didn't complain
They preferred their dads, to a trip to Spain.

Dolly Kershaw (10)
Hildenborough CE Primary School

HIDDEN TREASURES

Family and friends are my hidden treasures
They are really special to me
The world is full of hidden pleasures,
That sometimes you cannot see.

Hidden treasures are secret and precious
Private and forbidden, never to be heard,
A key should unlock the secrets of your life
Set them free like a flutter of a bird.

Victoria Keegan (10)
Hildenborough CE Primary School

HIDDEN TREASURES OF NATURE

Have you ever stopped to wonder,
What wonders nature has?
A rosy red apple or a beech tree, bark clad.
From a rainbow, a deer, a doe,
Or a beetle crawling low,
Or maybe a dog,
A mog,
Or even a hog.
Have you ever thought about
The life of a dewdrop?
Rolling on its solitary, silent journey, scaling a blade of grass
But Mother Nature can be cruel.
In winter bare,
Mother Nature's bounties wither,
Causing the silent sparrow to twitter!
In the summer warm,
By a butterfly does flitter,
Making the most of its two day life,
It's short life of mortal beauty,
On a winter morning break
No more the blue tit cheeps.

Max Richards (10)
Hildenborough CE Primary School

HIDDEN TREASURES

Travelling afar, across the open sea,
The sparkling sun sets the sea alight,
A most beautiful sight.
Fish diving, their shiny scales catching the light
And pushing it back, shining with all their might.
The dolphins jumping, squeak and say 'Follow me'
And off they go a-jumping throughout the open sea.
A hidden treasure . . .

Travelling afar, through the magical rainforest,
The soaking water sparkles against the sun filled with light,
A most beautiful sight.
Jaguars stalk the trees above,
Waiting to kill their prey in a silent binding love.
The butterflies, a thousand million, different coloured wings at rest
While the song bird sings.
A hidden treasure . . .

Rebecca Jenkins (11)
Hildenborough CE Primary School

HIDDEN TREASURES

Under a mountain far, far, far away,
Lie jewels and gold stored in a cavern,
Guarded by Smaug, a desolate beast,
With teeth like swords and fiery breath.
He guards all day with strength and bravery,
No fear, Smaug is on the move all day.
Dead bodies hang burnt on the slopes
Of the lonely mountain, Smaug's evil lair!

Until some people (well dwarfs and a Hobbit)
Come riding along and kill poor Smaug.
A long fought battle, many wounded
And the lonely mountain is lonely again
And all of the treasure is now hidden
Once more, under a tiny mound
Down tunnels and passages and through doors,
Of a little Hobbit hole!

Emily Miller (10)
Hildenborough CE Primary School

HIDDEN TREASURES

A photo album is full of hidden treasures,
All you have to do is open it,
And everything sparkles at you,
Like a chest full of gold.

This picture here's full of beauty,
No wonder, it's of me!
And here's one from last summer,
Here's my best friend, Eleanor.

Like a gliding bird,
Memories come flying back
Every picture is a key,
A key to a story,
That unfolds to reveal someone's life.

That's my family, in that picture there,
And the one with brown hair's me.

Elizabeth Berry (10)
Hildenborough CE Primary School

HIDDEN TREASURES - UNDERWATER TREASURE

'Hello, my name is
Octo the Octopus.
Do you have a name?
I have been told by
The king of the underworld
To keep this treasure safe!
You see I don't know what's inside,
Do you?
Well it could be some jewels,
Or an application to
Be the head of two schools.
Do you do what you are told to do?
I do!
Do you have treasures,
Like the king of underworld?
I do!
But I don't like telling anyone,
Because I want it to be
A mystery!'

Kirsty Coles (10)
Hildenborough CE Primary School

HIDDEN TREASURES - THE SNOWDROP

Buried in the ground all winter long,
Waiting for spring to come,
Awaiting the time
Like a star gradually appearing in the night sky,
Green shoots start thrusting themselves through the earth,
But the time is not right.
The shoots sink back down, disheartened,
Slowly it curls back up again, waiting bedraggled,
Waiting.

Then at last spring has come
And it rises above the ground, a beam of white light,
It rises in all its sparkling glory, a beautiful white bride.
But winter comes round again,
Its flowers die, its leaves go crusty and brown,
Like a defeated army slinking away,
It slides down underground,
Waiting for spring to come,
Waiting.

Eleanor Edwards (11)
Hildenborough CE Primary School

HIDDEN TREASURES

My hidden treasure is my cat
I know it sounds a bit silly.
Being an only child isn't easy
But when you've got such a good friend you feel as though
                                                                    you're not alone.
She welcomes me when I come home from school
She wakes me up when I'm half asleep.
She's called Rowan and I don't know why
As I walked along the narrow corridor at the RSPCA
I felt as though the cats were saying 'Pick me, pick me.'
But Rowan didn't say a thing, she was asleep!
When she woke she bashed against the transparent door
Almost saying 'They look nice.'
She feels soft like a carpet
She runs like a cheetah, charging up and down
She plays like a content baby
My hidden treasure is my cat.

Matthew Watts (10)
Hildenborough CE Primary School

SOUNDS, FEELINGS AND COLOURS

Silence,
A gaping black hole,
Death,
You lock your eyes in somebody else's
Nothing else matters,
Nothing.
A thought,
An idea,
A life,
It comes as a shock,
Your mind is fixed,
You try to control it but . . .
No.
Black and white,
Good and evil,
Yes and no.
The basis of life,
The only five things is their difference.
An explosion,
Explosions inside your head,
Sounds and colours flying around,
There is not always a bang.

Jack Witcomb (11)
Hildenborough CE Primary School

HIDDEN TREASURE - WISHING

I wish I was as fast as a car.
I wish I could fly like an eagle.
I wish I could play football for Arsenal.
I wish I could jump to the moon.
I wish I could play tennis like Tim Henman.
I wish I could eat whatever I wanted.

I wish I could swim like a fish.
I wish I had the map to Atlantis.
I wish I could breathe underwater.
I wish I could turn into any animal.
I wish I could find the hidden treasure.

Luke Hardy (10)
Hildenborough CE Primary School

MY TALENT

It was funny,
It was Sunday,
I was playing football,
I wasn't very good.
But then
I watched the ball
And it slowly sailed into the net -
I did it!
I scored!
With class!
I've found my talent!
That moment was great,
The joy,
The excitement,
All of it was great.
That night I had a dream
I was a striker for the school A team.
I was top scorer
And I won the Golden Boot Award.
Then I woke up.
When I was old enough
I did just that.

Nicholas Kennedy (11)
Hildenborough CE Primary School

HIDDEN TREASURE

Your imagination is so cool,
It can turn a swimming pool
Into the Pacific.
Your imagination is so great,
It can turn a dry sandwich on a plate
Into a feast terrific.

Your imagination is so fun,
It can turn no bright shining sun
Into a glorious day.
Your imagination is so big,
It can transform a wingless pig
Into an effortless flyer.

Your imagination is so swell,
So use it well,
It's a hidden treasure.

Laura Southall (11)
Hildenborough CE Primary School

HIDDEN TREASURES

As I cross the clear, beautiful, silky beach
My feet rebound off the stony rocks,
The sea is like a towel swishing side to side,
The seagulls squawking for food
And the wind swishing like a dart
Forcing itself to the board.

Jak Cook (11)
Hildenborough CE Primary School

A Hidden Treasure - My Football Dream

I was standing there gazing in the blue sky,
No one would pass to me
Or talk to me.
I was very angry and upset
Then I got the ball,
I was very excited,
I kicked it back,
Rachel passed it back
And I headed it straight in the goal.
I couldn't believe it, I actually scored a goal,
From then on I played my best,
Everyone liked me,
They passed and I would score,
Now I'm the best player on the team,
Now we are top.

Jade Williams (11)
Hildenborough CE Primary School

Happiness

Happiness is Heaven.
Happiness is a smile of a newborn baby.
Happiness is the chattering of robins in a tree.
Happiness is passing your driving test.
Happiness is your wedding day.
Happiness is a rose that has just blossomed.

Maxwell Oakley (10)
Hildenborough CE Primary School

HIDDEN TREASURES - THE WORLD OF NATURE

In the sea, the magnificent sea,
Tropical multicoloured fish, waggle and squirm
In the sea, the magnificent sea,
The water will shiver and twinkle.

In the rainforest, the delightful rainforest,
Wonderfully coloured toucans, flutter and glide.
In the rainforests, the delightful rainforests,
Trees of all kinds, will wave and swing.

This world of glorious treasures,
Let's be proud of all its wonders.

Natasha Wood (10)
Hildenborough CE Primary School

HIDDEN TREASURES - ANOTHER ME

The skateboard ollied with me
As the height from the ground grew.
'Wow' they shouted from the floor
'Ow' I screamed and I hit a police car.
CID is what they were
They pulled over and yelled 'Stop!'
But I didn't care
I jumped the car and off I went
I grinded some poles
I jumped with joy
Then leapt higher to the sky.
Skateboarding is so wicked
I wish all this wasn't a lie.

Michael Denton (10)
Hildenborough CE Primary School

I WISH . . .

I wish I could jump as high as the moon and see the stars glinting
                    and shining like little candles in the night sky.
I wish I could run as fast as Billy Whiz and win every race
                                      I ever entered.

I wish I could find,
I wish I could find,
I wish I could find a hidden treasure.

I wish I could swim like a fish and breathe underwater too, I could
                      explore under the sea all I liked.
I wish my drawings could come to life and I could play with them
                                      on weekends.

I wish I could find,
I wish I could find,
I wish I could find a hidden treasure.

I wish I could travel through time, I could see lots of people I never
                      knew and be good at history.
I wish I could fly like a bird, soar high in the sky and fly with
                                    the clouds.

I wish I could win,
I wish I could win,
I wish I could win this competition.

Sam Brown (10)
Hildenborough CE Primary School

GRENDEL SPEAKS

I don't want to be a Grendel
Everyone's scared of me
I have no friends and I never have had one
When I walk towards people everyone flees.
I mean, what's so scary about me?
I know I eat people
But do you really think I do it for fun?
If I had a friend none of the eating would have been done.
I have no name but Grendel
I have no money, none.
No clothes, no family, no friends
I'm the hairiest creature around
I go to the door of the hairdresser's
Watching the lucky humans having their hair cut
And I live down in the middle of a wood
In a big, lonely castle
I wish I was a human.

Bethany Thomas (10)
Marden Primary School

THE GRAND OLD OAK

Her hair in season changes
From green to mighty red.
In winter all her locks fall out
For they all turn brown and tumble down
Off her branching head.
Her eyes are soft with wrinkled skin
You see kindness lies within.
Animals play about her ground
And in her, no evil will be found.

Victoria Keith (11)
Marden Primary School

21st Century Poem

As I go along in my submarine
We're going slower, slower and slower.
I see bright, blazing, yellow fishes
In groups of ten for everyone to see
As they flow with the deep blue sea.
A huge blue whale making its path above our heads,
We come to a hole . . .
An octopus jumps out,
With its huge long suckers
Ready to grab at any moment.
There's a sunken ship
On the bottom of the seabed.
Pots that are ancient all cracked and crackled,
The sea urchins sticking on to them,
The texture of the sea makes me shiver within.

Jamie Sancto (10)
Marden Primary School

The Old Giant

Standing tall like a giant
With a lovely green fleece
Giving a home for his friends
Hugging anyone to keep them warm.
Dancing in the freezing wind
Not minding about anyone
He has a heart of gold
He can even be quite bold
Loving anyone who comes
This is the old giant.

Jonathan Funnell (10)
Marden Primary School

IF I COULD BOTTLE UP MY FEELINGS

If I could bottle up my feelings
I'd put my hope bottle on my bedside table for only me to see.
But if I'd bottle up my joy and delight
I'd put them on the window sill for the whole world to see.
If I'd bottle up my fear
I'd lock it up in the cellar and then
I'd quickly put my relief in a bottle and put it with hope.
Oh no! Hate has struck,
I'll find a big bottle
And then,
I'll lock it up forever and ever
For no one else to see.

James Boys (9)
Marden Primary School

THE GRENDEL'S POINT OF VIEW

In the forest in my cave,
Where I hide from my enemies,
Who did not let me join
Their merry feastings,
So I got revenge.
I blew down the great hall's doors,
I ate the people inside
While the ones that still survive
Screamed like death.
When all were killed I
Went back to my cave.

Richard Osborne (10)
Marden Primary School

THE STORM RAGES OUT

As the wind crashes against the garden wall
As the bricks on there are trying to fall
I'm next to the fire as the storm rages out
And certainly there's no people about.
I hear and feel the wind in the crack in the wall
And still the bricks are trying to fall.
The fence is being shaken
I hope it's not broken.
I'm trying not to fret
But the dog's getting wet
So I'm going outside to get him
I gently and gradually get to the door
I don't think I can take this any more.
So I ran up to bed
And rested my head
But in the morning everything was fine
It was just that silly imagination
Of mine.

Christian Hindley (11)
Marden Primary School

THE DIY MAN
(Inspired by The Highwayman)

The DIY man came riding up to the old inn door
He did it up real badly and it fell down on the floor.
It squashed poor Tom the Ostler and squeezed his guts quite tightly
His wife woke up in fright that night and said 'Tom, oh blimey!
That stupid DIY man, I'll have his guts for garters
Let's put him in the stocks and rain him with tomatoes!'

Alex Excell (10)
Marden Primary School

STARVE

To have no food,
To have no hope,
To have nothing to help you cope.
The nearest food is miles away
Your best chance is to walk all day.
Starving slowly with nothing to do
But I am not starving and neither are you.

Ruth Kelly (10)
Marden Primary School

TREES

One seed is planted
The tiny thing is slanted
As the weeks go by
The little seed begins to fly
Above the soil
Projecting out of the land
As it takes in its first breath of the world
The grown shoot begins to expand.

As the years go by
The young tree climbs up to the sky
Spreading its branches all over the wood
All alone the lonely tree stood.

Just imagine, this massive tree
Came from a seed
As big as a pea.

Rheanna Woodman (10)
Platt CE Primary School

TROPICAL WATERS

Down below the tropical waters,
Dolphins play.
Soon the sea horses and fish gather
To stay.
The coral bed so still,
As the shark moves in for the kill.
The coral reef, so gentle and calm,
The reef belongs in the world of a dolphin's palm.
The water sways and ripples foam
Then the dolphins get together to perform
As the starfish dance,
The sea horses start to prance.

Leigh-Anne Reardon (10)
Platt CE Primary School

THE SEA

The sea is a magical place
With all those brilliant colours
If you dive into the sea
It feels like you're in a dream.
You have the sea to yourself
No one is around, only the fishes
You could swim for ever.
The sea can change
From calm to rough
When it is calm or rough
It is out of this world.

Stephanie Lee (9)
Platt CE Primary School

DON'T CALL WILD ANIMALS RUDE NAMES TILL YOU'RE OUT THEIR WAY
(In the style of John Agard: Performance Poet)

Call armadillo stumpy legs,
Call armadillo rough head,
Call armadillo pointy tail,
Call armadillo scaly back.

> Call tiger dagger tooth,
> Call tiger beady golden eyes,
> Call tiger droopy whiskers,
> Call tiger swishy tail.

Call kangaroo big feet,
Call kangaroo rabbit ears,
Call kangaroo pouchy tum,
Call kangaroo jumpy feet.

> Call rhinoceros puffy toes,
> Call rhinoceros bumpy horn,
> Call rhinoceros dusty feet,
> Call rhinoceros leather skin.

Call wild animals all dem rude name,
> But better wait till you out their way.

Class D
Platt CE Primary School

SPACE

Sunrays, sunrays, shining on me,
That's what happens in space you see.
Moon beams, moon beams, beaming on me,
That's what happens in space you see.
Spinning, spinning, the Earth spins round,
The planet for which my rocket is bound.
Sunrays, moon beams, the Earth spinning round,
I like it in space, but it's safer on ground!

Joseph Gallant (11)
Platt CE Primary School

A NEW START

When the new year begins we feel small,
But now it has begun we can't go back.
Help us to grow and start again in life,
Let us forget the troubles and sins of the past year
And let us help the people who can't always start again.
Help us to try to keep peace rather than be violent,
Let us remember that no year is perfect -
Every year brings the unexpected and forsaken.

James Wagstaff (8)
Platt CE Primary School

HIDDEN TREASURE

Gleaming, golden box,
Shining like a ray of sunshine,
Glistening gems, sparkling jewels
Reflecting off the blazing sun.
Deep, dark secrets of the keyhole
A booming, bronze padlock.

A map leading to many dangers
Secret codes and messages baffling through your mind,
Scrawled paper,
Crinkled, ripped, torn, decayed,
Mysterious clues running through your head.
You're standing there, confused and depressed.

Worn peg-leg battered and bruised
Clothes tattered and torn
Long, bristly beard
Hanging from your chin.
Menacing pirate ship
Menace of seas.

Golden, sandy shores
Dangerous rocks jutting out
Brown, hairy coconuts
Dangling from the trees
Falling into seas.
Deadly traps to overcome
You better watch out, they might be near.

Keiran Yates (11)
St Anselms RC Primary School, Dartford

HIDDEN TREASURE

Cut-throat pirates searching for gold,
With their black patches over their eye,
Searching from their map
Not knowing where to look next,
Hanging skeletons in forbidden caves,
With old hanging daggers in their ribcage.

Searching long and hard for an old, battered box,
Just not knowing where to look next,
The glistening diamonds, the sparkling jewels,
So when they find it what will they do?
Digging deep holes, they found it,
The X on the map was surely true.

The box had an enormous bronze padlock,
But how would they open it?
This gleaming, golden box, what was this?
Was it gold or silver to spend
Or sparkling jewels to sell
Or was it just a lot of murky sand?

Sailing pirates in the menacing sea,
Leaving buried footprints in the sand,
Angry natives screaming in hate,
Washing on the musky sand, wooden boats,
It goes off in a flash of light,
And finds the chest is not to be opened.

Daniel Brooks (11)
St Anselms RC Primary School, Dartford

THE GHOSTLY GLOBE

I know somewhere and it's my secret
Where ghostly mists hover
And a silver moon is the only light.
Where chills crawl up my spine
And where icicles hang almost paralysed.
Plains of grass are covered with stiff frost.

I know somewhere and it's my secret
Where dreams are spoilt by sinister chills
And trees are covered with the purest snow.
Where a phantom wind throws clouds across the sky
Haunting music from a whistling wind spoils the deadly silence.

I know somewhere and it's my secret
Where snow whispers as it settles on a frosted grass,
And fog smothers spindly old bare trees
Where snow settles as if in secret.

I know somewhere and it's my secret
And it's a secret I'm sworn to keep.

Matthew Linnett (10)
St Anselms RC Primary School, Dartford

PEACE

Peace is love, joy and happiness
No enemies,
No sad feelings,
When will the friendship come to the world
To unite us together?
When will the doves fly over our heads?
When will those givers of peace hand out their love to the world
Of war and hate?

No bullying,
No fear of being hurt.
When will the rainbows,
The colours of peace
That will be the day
That I look forward to.

Joshua Perry (10)
St Anselms RC Primary School, Dartford

THE OLD TREASURE MAP

The old treasure map,
Torn and ripped,
With an X marking the spot,
Warning of danger
And anonymous fingerprints on it.

The old treasure map,
Well travelled
And looks like it has been through the wars
Twisted and turned up corner
And dirty smudged marks.

The old treasure map,
Clues to lead you anywhere
Or riddles that make you go mad,
They could lead you to a trap
Or maybe make you fall down a pit.

The old treasure map,
As old as me
Guiding us like a compass
And booming with adventure.

Samuel Whapshott (11)
St Anselms RC Primary School, Dartford

THE TREASURE CHEST

The shiny, golden treasure chest
Gleaming in the blazing sun
Gold and rusty hinge
Squeaking like a mouse.

Silver rounded coins
As shiny as a polished shield
Rubies as red as the evening sunset
Emeralds as green as a grassy field.

Diamonds sparkling within the chest
Like bubbling champagne
But on the outside hanging
Is the shimmering, bronze chain.

Perfect pearls as white as paper
Never-ending waves of dazzling jewels
The sparkling diamonds
Reflecting in the sun.

The yellowish, gold cups
Gleaming really bright.
The silver pieces shimmering
Like the moonlight.

Ruaidhri Marshall (10)
St Anselms RC Primary School, Dartford

THE TREASURE CHEST

The treasure chest is as shiny as a polished shield
It has rusted hinges on the back
A golden padlock dangles from the front.
Its hinges squeak like mice
The chest is as old as time
Glistening golden screws hang halfway out.

It has a never-ending flow of gold
The wooden edges are chipped
Its treasure is as big as the sea.
The rubies are as red as blood
And the gems are emerald green.
It's glistening padlock is as gold as the sun
The chest is old and brown.

Aaran Silva (11)
St Anselms RC Primary School, Dartford

THE TIGER

Prowling menacingly
Stalking its unexpecting prey,
Dark, fiery, orange,
Burnt black stripes
In the long grass it lay.

Pounce!
A vice-like grip,
A ferocious bite,
Blood dripping from its lip.

Bloodthirsty feast,
What a deadly terror,
An unstoppable beast,
Bloodstained teeth,
As sharp as blades.

Not so fast and furious,
Eyelids nearly closed,
One big yawn,
Resting its head,
Waiting for another day to dawn.

Tom Marsh (11)
St Anselms RC Primary School, Dartford

THE TREASURE CHEST

The sun reflects off the golden box
While the gold is hidden within
Covering the shiny jewels.
The golden box has a rusty lock
A rusty key will release the treasure.
Inside are emeralds as green as grass,
Rubies as red as blood,
Perfect pearls as white as the snow,
As shiny as a knight's sword.
The chest as strong as a knight's shield.
The chest is now open, the treasure is now free.
The gold shining as bright as the sun,
The silver as bright as the moon,
The rubies as red as blood,
Just like a sunset in the distance.
Diamonds sparkling within
Like bubbly champagne from a bottle.
A never-ending wave of dazzling jewels
Like stars shining in the night.

Louis Crowley (11)
St Anselms RC Primary School, Dartford

IF...

If your life has fallen apart,
Be prepared to start again.
It doesn't matter if you win or lose,
It's okay to have nothing.
Show faith in those around you
And be patient.
If life is just about you,
Show justice for other people.
If someone has hurt you always forgive and forget.

If you are stuck show perseverance,
When others do not.
If you get frightened,
Be brave and stand up to your fears.
If you become a slave to your dreams
Don't live on dreams alone.
Keep your cool, don't get stressed out
And if life becomes difficult
Show confidence.

Hayley Wilkinson (11)
St Anselms RC Primary School, Dartford

HIDDEN TREASURE

The deep blue ocean
Washes upon the sandy shores of the beach.
While the sun shines all day
The treasure chests waits
And waits to be opened.
All the jewels, gold and silver
Shine in the blazing sun
Through holes in the chest.
The dark, gloomy cave
Waits to spring its lethal death traps
On the hopeless.
The coconuts drop down
From the tree like rain from a cloud.
'Ahoy maties!' yelled one of the pirates
Walking on the shore
With an old wooden leg.
Two pirates walk to their doom
In the deep, dark cave.
Who knows if they will return?

Stephen Hutchins (11)
St Anselms RC Primary School, Dartford

My Hidden Treasure

Here I am
On the secret island
Where I hope to find my treasure.
I am standing on
The golden, sandy shore.
The waves from the sea
Are as tall as me.
I start to dig
By some dangerous rocks
On my map this is where
I marked my red cross.
I dig and dig
Until my spade hits
Something solid.
I pull it out and there it is
My treasure.
I stare down
At a gleaming, gold box
Reflecting on the burning sun.
The light is so bright
It is blinding
But I don't care
I've found my treasure.

Sian Bull (11)
St Anselms RC Primary School, Dartford

IF . . .

If you put your trust in others
Don't doubt others of the crime they didn't do
Others will put their trust in you.
Don't hate those who hate you.

If your life has fallen apart
Be prepared to start again.
Just because someone hates you
You don't have to hate them too.
Be brave and stand up to your fears.
Help others who are falling down.
Don't be ruled by your thoughts.
Listen to other opinions.

It doesn't matter if you win or lose.
Be realistic in what you think or say
Keeping your temper at all times.
Show perseverance
While others are giving up.
Believe in yourself when nobody else does
Show faith in those around you.

Don't be boastful.
Show friend to people.
Always show forgiveness.
Forget and not hold grudges against people.

Emmanuel Ahamefula (10)
St Anselms RC Primary School, Dartford

THE WIZARD

There he is fast and furious
Shooting through the sky like
A shooting star.
He is sly and cunning.

They're back at the castle
Making potions, he stood
In front of the jet-black cauldron
Using spell words from the old,
Tattered and torn spellbook.

As he walked around the castle
He dragged his long, white beard
In front of him and dragging his
Sparkling, purple cloak behind him.
It seems magical from my point of view.

An owl hooting, it is as wise
As the wizard himself.
One flick of his wand
And everything is destroyed.

He poured the potions into
A painted, glass bottle and
Brought it up to the sparkling, mysterious crystal ball
And placed it into it.
That's when I knew he was a wizard.

Laura Harney (10)
St Anselms RC Primary School, Dartford

IF...

If you can keep your patience
When others around you cannot.
If you can keep your cool
And never get stressed out.
If you can put your trust in people
Never show them any doubt.
If you have dreams
Don't let them lead your life.
If you have thoughts
Don't become a slave to them.
If you be brave and stand up to your fears
You can help others who are falling down.
If you don't hate those who hate you
By showing friendship, caring and sharing.
If you show perseverance
While others are giving up.
If you show forgiveness
While others can't forgive and forget.
If you keep your temper
While everyone is losing their heads.
If it is okay to have nothing
Nothing can be a good beginning.
If you let bad times go
Have a good time by starting afresh
And what is more you will have succeeded!

Celina Quinn (10)
St Anselms RC Primary School, Dartford

THE WIZARD

A long, white, twisting beard,
Flowing robes draped behind him
As he picked an old, tattered spellbook up
And looked down at his potent potions.
He stretches out his hands,
He weaves his hands above
The jet-black cauldron
Prepared for anything.
He looks down with a sneaky smile on his face
His pointy wand lying patiently on the floor.
I could see his half-moon glasses,
His old, crooked fingers
Cover his round face.
I knew this man was different from you and me
His scarred, wrinkled hands
Weaved once again over another jet-black cauldron.
His hooting owl
Sitting, grabbing hold of his weird-coloured cloak
His peculiar manner in which he acts!
Standing there quite content.
Suddenly,
A crash!
A poof!
There in his hands was the most amazing thing,
A sparkly silver and a glittery gold
An extraordinary thing, a crystal ball.
He rubbed it gently
Bang!
Magically he had vanished,
I wondered if I'd see him again.

Emma Pearce (10)
St Anselms RC Primary School, Dartford

AN UNSTOPPABLE BEAST

Strolling through the long, blazing grass,
Is a fearsome, deadly animal.
He's fast and he's furious
And he's bloodthirsty.

Eyes like red-hot fire,
Scanning the land for prey,
A magnetic stare is fixed to a warthog,
His eyes are going nowhere.

Teeth as sharp as daggers,
As solid as a rock.
His white teeth will soon be bloodstained
As he gets closer and closer.

Claws like razors,
Soaring through the long grass.
It would take one deadly pounce
And you wouldn't see that hog again.

As strong as ten men,
He's so powerful,
He's got a vice-like grip,
An unstoppable beast.

The blazing streaks of black
Sit on his dark, fiery, orange back,
Creeping slowly closer and closer
His mouth watering like mad.

He pounces,
The tiger has caught his prey.

Lara Wrubel (11)
St Anselms RC Primary School, Dartford

HIDDEN TREASURE

Ships with a crew of pirates,
Black eyepatches
As dark as the night,
Long, weathered beards,
Worn peg legs.
Treasure maps
With burnt, torn edges.
The ship moves to the island
Met by palm trees,
Brown, hairy coconuts,
And golden, yellow sand,
Green trees
And on we go.
Through the tropical rainforest.
Two steps to the left,
Six steps forward,
Death traps everywhere.
Arrows flying,
The ground crumbling,
Rotting carcasses of pirates.
We stop for a drink
From a freshwater spring
And on we go.
X marks the spot.
Slowly we dig
Uncovering a smooth,
Wooden treasure chest.
On the boat,
Home we go
To reveal our prize.

Kevin Coen (10)
St Anselms RC Primary School, Dartford

THE RUBY-RED FOX

As the morning sun rises
The ruby-red fox appeared
From a hole in the green, dewy ground.
Its eyes scanned the area to see if breakfast
Was hiding beneath the grass.
A rustle sounded
As the bell echoed from the village.
The cunning fox crawled in slow motion
Like a newly born hedgehog.
Nothing rustled
Not even the well-hidden prey.
The aroma hit the fox's highly sensitive nose,
It was a strong, healthy, young buck.
Slowly but cautiously the fox's magnetic eyes
Fixed on the young buck.
Even though the long, dewy grass was blocking his view.
Suddenly . . .
The fox's razor teeth glinted
Its claws dug into the ground
The innocent, young buck hopped nearer
Like a lamb to the slaughter.
The fox dug out its sharp claws and
Dashed towards the young buck like lightning.
Unexpectedly the young buck flew around
And disappeared down a hidden hole
Like a magician's disappearing act.
Sadly the poor fox turned, confused and disappointed
And scuttled back to his den
Once again.

Bethany Campbell (11)
St Anselms RC Primary School, Dartford

HIDDEN TREASURE

On a desert island
Buried under the golden sand
Lies the tattered treasure chest
Which for years has never been found.

Its booming, bronze padlock,
Its rusty, steel chain,
The deep, dark secrets of the keyhole
Which lock out the dreams within.

It looks over and out to the seashore
It sees decaying planks of wood from a shipwreck.
The grey glistening rocks by the seashore
Looking dented, battered and bruised.

The chest's chain is gleaming,
Shining like a ray of sunlight.
People still search for its treasures
Like the jewels hidden inside.

When I say jewels I mean diamonds,
Shining gems in the clasps of rings,
Gold and silver coins and bracelets,
Glittering crystals in the hands of a necklace.

The only clue to its whereabouts
Is the map with unsolvable riddles,
But you have to overcome deadly traps,
So if you come looking for this special chest
You must be prepared to die.

It looks like no man will find it
So don't go and look yourself.
Even though it is tempting,
Do not risk your life.

Siobhan Martin (11)
St Anselms RC Primary School, Dartford

PEACE

Peace is about love,
Peace is about friendship,
Peace is where nobody fights
And everyone gets along.

God and Jesus,
The givers of peace,
They helped everyone
And there was no fear in the world.

There should be silence,
No violence,
Everyone friends,
No one foes.

In the world there should be . . .
No racism,
No arguments
And no bullying.

A flickering candle
Is a calming flame,
The light of Christ
It shows us the way.

I have a dream of a world
There is no fear,
No enemies
Or no sadness.

In this world I dream of . . .
'Peace rules!'

James Aylwin (10)
St Anselms RC Primary School, Dartford

PIRATE TREASURE

Under the sea or buried in the ground
There is some treasure that cannot be found.
Pirates come from lands afar,
Searching here and there, near and far.
With their black eye patches as dark as the night,
Always on the look out for treasure in sight.
Their long, bristly beards and feathered parrots,
Sit on their shoulders and is orange as a raw carrot.
In their scarred, scary hand they hold a treasure map
It's crinkled and ripped with so many flaps.
Secret codes and messages that baffle your mind,
The big, black X shows you the treasure you're trying to find.
It has golden, sandy shores which cover the ground
The map leads them to an island, where the treasure will be found.
The bright, blue waves as tall as grown men
The sandy shore sparkles like glistening gems.
Skeletons of pirates lead up to the treasure
Like a bony path it is too long to measure.
Pieces of wood washed up on the shore,
Deep, dark caves with secrets for ever more.
Anonymous footprints buried deep in the sand,
Brown, hairy coconuts all over the land.
When you finally find the treasure chest, the gleaming, golden box
With its booming, brown padlock.
The old, battered, wooden box
Containing the best
Sparkling jewels and precious pearls
Shining silver coins only fit for Earls.
Glistening gems, oh what can it be?
Oh why, oh why, they forgot the key!

Miriam Adisa (11)
St Anselms RC Primary School, Dartford

THE TREASURE CHEST

Golden like the sun
Glittering and glinting
Reflecting off the blazing sun.
The wooden edges as rough as a pine tree
Deep, dark secrets deep inside.
Old, rusty lock waiting to be broken
Bronze padlock, old as time.
As shiny as a polished shield,
Misty lock,
Dark, long keyhole.
Perfect pearls as white as bones,
Full of gold like a sea full of fish,
Emeralds as green as lush grass,
Rubies red as blood,
Silver, rounded coins,
Diamonds sparkling like bubbly champagne.
With a never-ending wave of jewels
That dazzle in the sunlight.
Rusty hinges squeaking like a mouse,
Gems and jewels
From faraway lands
Like rubies for
A Raja, the king of the Indians.
Crystals dazzling
In the sun
And the moonlight.
This treasure chest will be opened,
But not now,
But later
In the future.

Gregory White (10)
St Anselms RC Primary School, Dartford

THE TREASURE CHEST

The old worn chest
As rough as sandpaper
The cold padlock waiting to be broken.
Cold, rusty hinges squeaking like a mouse
The wood seems like it's going to snap.

Rubies as red as blood,
Silver pieces shimmering like the moon,
Shimmering bronze chains
Never-ending wave of dazzling jewels
Gold coins shining like stars.

Sparkling diamonds, glittering and glinting
Emeralds as green as the lush grass,
Perfect pearls as white as snow,
The jewels as shiny as a knight's new sword
Diamonds sparkling within like bubbling champagne.

It's as old as time
The treasure chest lost for years waiting to be found
Any woman's dream to have this.

Sophie Randall (11)
St Anselms RC Primary School, Dartford

THE TREASURE CHEST

There is a rusty, wooden box
As rough as sandpaper
It's waiting to be broken
By men far and near.

The padlock shines
As gold as the gleaming sun
Waiting for the key to go inside
An opening to the wonders it holds within.

It holds rubies as red as blood,
Emeralds as green as the lush grass,
Pearls as white as the clouds above,
All waiting to come out.

The wooden box as old as time
Held by rusty hinges
That squeaks like a mouse,
The box with deep, dark secrets inside.

Kelvin Canty (10)
St Anselms RC Primary School, Dartford

FAIRYLAND

Beyond, beyond the wardrobe door
Fairyland is waiting for you
Ruby-red stream
Glittering castle
Friendly animals
Birds singing songs.

Beyond, beyond the wardrobe door
Flowers smell of chocolate
Floating lollipops
Fizzy sweets
Warm bright sun.

Beyond, beyond the wardrobe door
Animals play games
Everyone is happy
Monkeys swing on trees
Otters do tricks.

Hannah Williams (9)
St James' RC Primary School, Bromley

DARK SPACE

I have heard of gold jewels far away,
I know what to do, I must not stay.
I must go and find what I've treasured most,
And then I can celebrate with a lovely hot roast.

I know where the jewels are, they're up in dark space
At this rate it will take a very quick and big pace.
I know what to do, I must be very brave,
Then when I come home, I can sit by the pool and sunbathe.

I've hired a rocket, I must go now,
I might even get back in time for the January sale.
It's going to take long, it will be very far,
The only trouble is, is dodging the stars.

I have got in my rocket, ready to go,
I just hope on the way it doesn't start to snow!
I have got this far, there's no going back,
Because my mates might lose their temper and start to attack!

I'm in dark space and I can see the moon,
At this rate I might get to Earth just before noon.
I'm on the moon and can see the jewels,
And look for my dad some shiny new tools!

Matthew Pettifer (10)
St James' RC Primary School, Bromley

MY BUNNY

I have a little bunny, Ole is his name
He doesn't like to play out in the rain.
He plays out when it's sunny
And heads a ball, that's funny.

He's brown and white and fluffy
His tail is short and puffy
His whiskers are long and thin
And he has a hutch for living in.

Louise Allen (8)
St James' RC Primary School, Bromley

THE TERRIFIC TREASURE

'You get this treasure,' my boss said,
'Or you'll all end up without your head.'
'But what can this thing really do?'
Said Micky Martin, Chris and Drew.
'Stop your moaning, stop complaining,
Soon it'll start to be raining.'
And so we set off with a map,
To find where the treasure sat.
And we walked along the ground,
To where the treasure could be found.
And then we went into the lair,
To get the treasure, beautiful rare.
We opened up the treasure chest,
To see where the treasure rest.
We picked it out the golden sand,
And passed it round from hand to hand.
Then went back to the boss' place
For we had won the treasure race.
And sat down to biscuits and for cheese,
For our boss was really pleased.
We went to bed and slept like logs
And cuddled up to our dogs.
And fell fast asleep.

Thomas Eves (10)
St James' RC Primary School, Bromley

FIVE BLACK CATS

Five black cats
sitting on a wall
one jumped off
because he was too tall.

Four black cats
waiting for their food
one didn't get any
because he was too rude.

Three black cats
running from dogs
one ran off
he was a clever clogs.

Two black cats
waiting for their kippers
one got lonely and
ran off with Grandad's slippers.

One black cat
left upon the wall.
He's the black cat
who has it all.

Luke Brook (9)
St James' RC Primary School, Bromley

BLUE BOY BASIL ALLEN RIP

My budgie Blue Boy
was a very special thing.
He didn't really do much
and he couldn't really sing.
He chirped a lot
and flapped about
just to stretch his wings.

Now he's dead and gone to Heaven
and I'm as sure as I can be,
that he's flying high up in the clouds
and looking down at me.
Flying here and flying there
and singing happily.
My Blue Boy Basil Allen RIP.

Rachel Allen (8)
St James' RC Primary School, Bromley

FELIX

My baby brother,
He's only one-year-old,
He's walking on two feet now,
And becoming very bold.
He's very energetic,
He loves to scream and shout,
Playing games and running around is what he's all about.
He makes me very happy,
He always has a smile,
He waves me off to school each day,
I walk it . . . it's only a mile!
We have a bath together each night,
Before he goes to bed,
I love to watch him sleeping,
Resting his weary head.
But most of all I love him,
Because he's brought to me,
Such happiness and laughter,
He completes my family.

Charles Turner (8)
St James' RC Primary School, Bromley

THE HIDDEN TREASURE

I was on a mission to find some gold
And I bet it will just be sold.
The map will take me far and wide,
To the highest ever tide.
The treasure of the sea.

The map was very badly torn,
And battered to pieces, like some corn.
I packed my bag, I was ready to go,
The bag was full so I would be slow.
The treasure of the sea.

I was outside the door, I was on my way,
Won't I return or will I may?
I was on my way there's no turning back
And I prayed there was nothing I did lack,
The treasure of the sea.

The map found me up a mountain,
I was very thirsty, but there was no fountain.
I was getting close to the deep blue sea,
So the one who gets the treasure must be me.
The treasure of the sea.

I saw the treasure laying nearby,
The treasure was surely mine.
I bought it home to my family,
Me and them were so happy.
The treasure that was mine.

Joshua Hughes (10)
St James' RC Primary School, Bromley

FRED THE BIRD

Fred, Fred, Fred the bird,
Loved to eat his lemon curd,
Chocolate buttermilk and cream
Stopped that bird from being mean,
Chocolate and crisps, all so nice,
He bought them all from 'Birdfood Price'.

Bread and jam, ever so yummy,
Cheese and ham, oh so scrummy,
Spaghetti Bolognese and pasta,
You couldn't get such good food faster,
A couple of chips and tomato sauce
Kept Fred's voice from being hoarse,
Roast beef and roast potatoes,
Salad cream and three tomatoes.

A few more foods that Fred quite likes,
Some more he thinks are rather nice,
Has to include his grandma's tea
And his aunty Mable's hot coffee.
Stilton cheese and mozzarella,
A slice of toast topped with nutella.
But even though all these foods
Keeps Fred in quite a good mood,
The thing that Fred likes much more than cheese
Is to gobble up a bunch of seeds.

So I ask you, on Fred's behalf,
To keep his table on the path.
Do not change his diet to cheese,
Just keep it as birdseed please!

Ruth Andrews (11)
St James' RC Primary School, Bromley

SPACE

When I went to space one night,
Boy, did I get a fright,
I was on my way to the moon
Oh I hope I get there soon.

When I went to space again
I saw some shiny stars,
The aliens were having a race
I think they're heading for Mars.

When at last I arrived in space
I saw the Milky Way.
Wow, it looks fantastic,
I wish I could stay.

Nicholas Greenwood (8)
St James' RC Primary School, Bromley

DREAM

I dream of a land far, far away
Where dragons feed on men
Where lava flows like molten iron
And towering mountains stand.

I dream of a land far, far away
Where the moon does never set
Where it is night, not noon, not day
Not eve, not morn, not dusk.

I dream of a land far, far away
I stand face to face with a dragon
I scream so loud that he runs away
And I wake with a burn in my heart.

Harry McAleer (9)
St James' RC Primary School, Bromley

THE SENSIBLE DAY AT THE BEACH

I *smell* the salty sea
As its waves crash onto the beach.

I *taste* a chocolate ice cream
While it melts in the sun.

I *see* flags on sandcastles
Blowing in the wind.

I *hear* the sound of seagulls
That soar through the sky.

I *feel* the sand
Underneath my feet.

Drip, drop it's raining
It's time to go home.

Charlotte Georgina Weeks (8)
St James' RC Primary School, Bromley

DREAM LAND

Beyond, beyond the wardrobe door
The river twinkles
Lovely light blue sky
Bright yellow sun that shines
The birds sing a joyful song
The people are kind and caring
Stars shimmer in the night sky
The moon brightens the land
Dolphins twirl in the shimmering sea
The fish glide in the deep blue ocean.

Molly Grace Fathers (8)
St James' RC Primary School, Bromley

DOZY DOGS

Five dozy dogs
running around
one got bored
so he went to the pound.

Four dozy dogs
laying on the chair
one got off and
left a lot of hairs.

Three dozy dogs
wagging their tail
one got off
because he looked pale.

Two dozy dogs
barking all day
one did not like it
so he went away.

One dozy dog
laying in the sun
so he went away
and then there was none.

No dozy dogs
left in the park
perhaps they will come back
wait until they bark.

Grace McCarthy (8)
St James' RC Primary School, Bromley

PIRATES

One, two
The captain's
Got the flu.

Three, four
Knock on the
Cabin door.

Five, six
Catch some
Fish.

Seven, eight
Call the
Ship's mate.

Nine, ten
'He's ill
Again!'

Eleven, twelve
The captain yelled.

Thirteen, fourteen,
Pirates fighting.

Fifteen, sixteen,
It was frightening.

Jack Harper (8)
St James' RC Primary School, Bromley

MAN U

Striker scores
Now it's 2-1
Come on everyone
Let's have fun.

Goalie saves
Kicks the ball
Then the fans say
You are cool.

Midfield lobs
Passes to star
Beckham kicks
Over the bar.

Ref's whistle blows
Ninety minutes are up
Crowd shouts hurrah!
Man U held the cup.

John Hatch (8)
St James' RC Primary School, Bromley

CHAOS LAND

Beyond, beyond the wardrobe door
Treacherous tornadoes
Spinning, spinning, whooshing, whooshing
Faster than the speed of light
Waiting to transport you to the centre of the vortex
Where raging lava waits
Ready to swallow you up
As it stands as huge as a mountain
Prepared to confront you.

Robert Adams (9)
St James' RC Primary School, Bromley

MY FAVOURITE ANIMALS

Panthers are black as midnight
Panthers' fur is soft as velvet
Panthers are as swift as the wind
Panthers drink from moonlit waters
Panthers' claws are as sharp as a knife
Panthers' eyes are as bright as the sun.

Eagles' eyes are blazing yellow
Eagles are called birds of prey
Eagles swoop down from the sky
Eagles can see far and wide.

Snakes are vicious creatures
Snakes open their mouths to grab their prey
Snakes' fangs are poison-full
Snakes' eyes are diamond-shaped
Snakes slither through the grass
Snakes coil for a sleep.

Liam Docherty (8)
St James' RC Primary School, Bromley

THE PEACE MAKING MAN

The peace making man
Held out his hand
To shake it
With someone else.

The other man
Was Jackie Chan
Who was paranoid
And wouldn't touch him.

Leo Wyard (10)
St James' RC Primary School, Bromley

ANIMAL ANTICS

Seven dopey donkeys,
Racing round the track.
One jumped over the railings
And the rider fell off its back.

        Six mischievous monkeys,
        Itching everywhere,
        One saw a banana
        But got frightened by a bear.

Five angry alligators,
Waiting for their lunch,
One saw a fish
And it started to munch.

        Four hyper hippos
        Splashing in the river,
        One got out,
        And it started to shiver.

Three rude rhinos
Stamping their feet,
They then started charging
And got angry in the heat.

        Two gigantic giraffes,
        Looking around,
        One saw a person
        Down on the ground.

One diving dolphin
Splashing in the sea.
It saw a killer whale
And it was looking for its tea.

Emily Hobbs (8)
St James' RC Primary School, Bromley

THE GUNNERS WIN

The Gunners kick off
As the ref's whistle blows.
The crowd cheers
As Henry careers
Down the centre - off he goes.

The Devils are mad
Beckham tackles badly
The ref shouts
The tension mounts
While Henry cries out madly.

Pires picks up the ball
And races past Veron
Crosses in low
Campbell with the blow
Shoots hard and scores - on the run.

Half-time finally comes
The Gunners' fans are singing:
'Down the Devils
Up the Gunners
The trophy's there for the winning!'

The Devils break through
With the ball at Blanc's feet
He hits hard
'*Goal*!' he roared
As the scores finally meet.

The last chance suddenly comes
As Bergkamp has a shot
It swerves high
Into the net
Arsenal add to the trophies they've got!

Patrick Bunnage (10)
St James' RC Primary School, Bromley

THE BIG RACE

3, 2, 1 the race has begun,
To find the secret treasure,
The treasure is lots of emeralds,
Rub in gold and pleasure,
But to find all this treasure,
You have to be very clever.

To find the treasure,
You have to have a map,
And reading this map is hard,
That is why you need a specialist,
To read the map for everyone
And to make some buns.

Now we started to look for the map,
The most important thing in the race,
It could take minutes, it could take hours,
It could even take days.
I just hope we don't lose
Or we'll have to pay.

Is it in the long grassed field,
Or up a very tall tree?
Is the map in bushes,
Or up in the very high sky?
There it is! By that owl,
I wonder how I'll get it down?

I know, I'll climb up that ladder
I've got the map, now time to get the treasure.
The map says it's near,
Its glimmer, the pressure.
There's the treasure shining bright
We've won the race, yes! the pride.

Dominic Makepeace (10)
St James' RC Primary School, Bromley

SIX CRAFTY CROCS

Six crafty crocs
Coming out to play
What new adventures
Has the world in store today?

Five crafty crocs
Creeping through the trees
Warming up their scaly skin
In the summer breeze.

Four crafty crocs
Waiting for their prey
Wondering what animal
They'll have for lunch today.

Three crafty crocs
Swimming in the lake
Backstroke, breaststroke
Or any they can make.

Two crafty crocs
Climbing up the stairs
Scrambling into jim-jams
They say their goodnight prayers.

One crafty croc
Hiding in the covers
Hugging his teddy bear
Waiting for his mother.

No crafty crocs
Sitting having fun
For all of them are safe in bed
As down goes the sun.

Roberto Battista (9)
St James' RC Primary School, Bromley

UNDERNEATH THE SURFACE

Underneath the surface,
Where under treasure awaits,
Oh, hurry let's get moving,
You don't want to be late?

The necklace holds the power,
To enslave all mankind
So when I get the necklace,
Together the world shall bind.

Rubies of red,
Sapphires of blue,
Emerald and diamond
And garnets too!

So down beneath the surface,
To the lost city,
Where the riches were scattered
Oh what a pity.

So when I go diving
As I will some day,
I'll make peace for the world,
It'll be that way.

Catherine Preston (10)
St James' RC Primary School, Bromley

THE HORSE WAVE

There's magic in the air
There's treasures in the sea
The horse wave is a wonder to see
The galloping surf rushes to the shore
They reach the sand and run no more.

The shore whispers to the herd
They rear their heads to greet the shore
Faces appear through the foaming sea
They gallop to the shore once more
To meet their destiny.

Emily Loftus (11)
St James' RC Primary School, Bromley

FIVE BARKING DOGS

Five barking dogs
Barking more and more
One got a headache
Then there were four.

Four barking dogs
Fitting with a bee
One was stung
Then there were three.

Three barking dogs
Shouting boo
One lost his voice
Then there were two.

Two barking dogs
Having an ice bun
One was full
Then there was one.

One barking dog
Went for a run
Had enough fun
Then there were none.

Marie Wallis (11)
St James' RC Primary School, Bromley

I Like Football

I like to watch football games
I like to see the players' names
I like to see lots of scoring
otherwise it's really boring.

I like to hear the fans cheering
but I don't like the fans jeering.
I like to see the goalkeeper saving
but not the goalkeeper lazing.

I like the half-time drink which
helps the players think.
I like the boo of the tackle
as the crowds cackle.

I like it when the game stops
when the team pops with screams and yells.
The losing team say this is hell.

The ref breathes a sigh of relief
He survives another game without losing his teeth.
I like the results and Match of the Day
Gary and his men wish they could still play!

John Pereira (11)
St James' RC Primary School, Bromley

Deep, Deep Down

Deep, deep down
At the bottom of the sea
Much too deep
For you and for me
Where the octopus roam
And the fish swim free.

I would like to go and see
But it's much too deep for me
But I have a friend called Willie
Who I'll go and see
For you and for me
But only after my tea.

Taylor Norman (10)
St James' RC Primary School, Bromley

MY FRIENDS

My friends
Are the most important people to me
I can trust them
For eternity
We do funny things together
And look after each other when we are under the weather
We will be best friends forever!

My friends make me laugh
My friends make me smile
We hang out in a gang
And sometimes we're wild
We might act loud
And sometimes scary
But really we're just as angelic as a fairy!

We might have fights
That end in tears
But we're best friends
So we have no fears!

Stephanie Arch (11)
St James' RC Primary School, Bromley

DOLPHINS IN THE SEA

Dolphins in the sea,
Swimming all around,
Jumping in and out,
Splashing with their tails.

See the dolphins jump,
In and out they surf,
Happy and free,
Oh to be a dolphin,
With all the world to see.

See the dolphins glide,
Singing as they go,
See the merry dancing,
Going with the flow.

Oh to be a dolphin
Happy and free!

Amy Ewen (10)
St James' RC Primary School, Bromley

SPORT

Football, netball, hockey too
Are all the sports I love to do.

Swimming, running, tennis too
But whatever the sport it's good
For you.

Football is my favourite sport
I play in defence and don't get caught.
I pass to the middle from the corner pole.
To let my teammate score a goal!

Charlotte Rafferty (10)
St James' RC Primary School, Bromley

SQUIRREL

I'm a little squirrel
On the high top trees
Looking down at the nuts
Among the autumn leaves.
I'm so graceful with my grey fur coat
When I jump I look like I'm on a boat,
Sailing through the trees instead of the seas.
But suddenly I'm falling, I'm falling and
I didn't get a warning!
Then *bump* I'm a lump
On the autumn floor.
But where are the leaves?
Where are the trees?
Oh! It was only a dream!

Hannah Meadowcroft (10)
St James' RC Primary School, Bromley

FOOTBALL

Football, what a wonderful thing
It makes the crowd shout and sing.
The red and blacks are the ones I follow
Hey, red card! The ref's head must be hollow!

Hear comes Bergkamp, takes a shot
Yes, Barthez saves, that shot seemed red-hot.
Wait, a shot from Keane
He scores - what a dream!

1-0 the final score
We win but we should have scored more.
Football, what a simple name
For a brilliant game!

Niall Wharton (11)
St James' RC Primary School, Bromley

HIDDEN TREASURES

There are probably treasures inside of me,
that no one else has found,
just like the precious artefacts,
all hidden underground.

Maybe I'm good at netball,
perhaps I'm perfect at art,
I might be great in drama,
do you think I'll get the main part?

No one knows what their's are yet,
but they'll be out pretty soon,
when you're not expecting it,
they'll arrive with a *boom!*

Rebecca Reidy (10)
St James' RC Primary School, Bromley

THIS POEM

This poem's not long,
This poem's not short,
This poem's not sold,
This poem's not bought.

This poem can't sing,
This poem can't talk,
This poem can't dance,
This poem can't walk.

This poem won't scream,
This poem won't roar,
This poem won't shout,
This poem's a bore.

Rachel Pritchard (11)
St James' RC Primary School, Bromley

SNEAKY SNAKES

Six sneaky snakes wriggling far and near
one popped into the pub to have a can of beer.

Five sneaky snakes have extraordinary motions
sun gleaming in winter and snowflakes rubbed in lotions.

Four sneaky snakes getting the cane
why? Teachers like that they'll never be the same.

Three sneaky snakes trying to win this competition
crept up on the judges to find they had a mission.

Two sneaky snakes very undersize
went to primary school but couldn't do their ties.

One sneaky snake loves incredible exciting action
wriggled to the soccer match and ended up in traction.

No sneaky snakes to be seen anywhere
Perhaps they'll come back to seek the fresh air.

Catherine Dow (9)
St James' RC Primary School, Bromley

WHY DO I HAVE TO TIDY MY ROOM?

What are we doing for fun today?
Can I go outside and play?
Why do I have to tidy my room?
I'd rather be dead and locked in a tomb.

Why is it important to see the floor?
It's not my mess, it's my brother's I'm sure.
I could escape and fly to the moon.
Oh why do I have to tidy my room?

Simon Brindley (8)
St James' RC Primary School, Bromley

THE RARE JEWEL

To find the treasure,
Which would be a pleasure.
Oh how I wish to find the jewel.
Where is the place?
To find this map along a race.
Why do we have to eat our gruel?

We found the map worn,
All crumbled and torn,
It was in a cave,
Our first destiny was here,
We were really very near?
Our team were extremely brave.

They found a boat,
Which nearly took us afloat,
And we sailed across the sea.
We saw lots of fish
And one even landed on a dish,
But the fish wasn't bigger than me.

We reached the island of the rare jewel,
Why does everyone have to be so cruel?
I found the jewel's cross,
And we dug up the earth,
But not to find a curse . . .
The rare jewel.
       The diamond!

Rachel Baldwin (9)
St James' RC Primary School, Bromley

HIDDEN TREASURE

Hidden treasure under the sea,
Hidden treasure what can it be?
Is it jewellery?
Is it money?
I don't know what it can be,
But maybe you can tell me?

Hidden treasure under the sea,
Hidden treasure where can it be?
Is it left?
Is it right?
I don't know where it can be
But maybe you can tell me?

Hidden treasure under the sea,
Hidden treasure whose can it be?
Is it bandits?
Is it pirates?
I don't know whose it can be,
But maybe you can tell me?

Hidden treasure under the sea,
Hidden treasure where can it be?
Here it is,
There it is,
I know whose it is,
     It's mine.

Kelly-Ann Marrington (10)
St James' RC Primary School, Bromley

WHAT ARE YOU DOING IN HERE?

My favourite room is white and blue,
It's big and bright with a loo,
In the middle is a four-poster bed,
Where I like to rest my head.
I try on the clothes from every drawer,
Throw them around onto the floor.
I love the lipsticks, orange and pink,
The perfume smell, well actually stink.
On the wall is Westlife and A1,
They're okay but I prefer Sum41,
I like to count the football team
Until I hear that dreaded scream,
I know shoe's going to find me here,
But soon it will be mine, just one more year.
I love this place, which is to be mine soon,
But for now it's my sister's room.

Jessica Watkins (11)
St James' RC Primary School, Bromley

THE HIDDEN TREASURE

I'm on a mission to find a golden cup,
I'm going with my pup.
In the cave it's dark
We sing, I must say I am in shock.
I spill Fanta down my sock.

The lock opened, there was a map,
So over the hill they go.
Through the jungle, they must go,
Into the boat and through the cave
And say, 'There's the treasure, I think.'

On the map it said through the cave we must go.
Over the hill and through fields,
Across the desert into the water
And there was the golden cup.

Joe Hall (9)
St James' RC Primary School, Bromley

BOUNCY BUNNIES

Five bouncy bunnies
bounding in a row
one fell over
and hurt his toe.

Four bouncy bunnies
skiing down a slope
one tripped over
a very long rope.

Three bouncy bunnies
jumping on a bridge
one bouncy bunny
jumped over the ridge.

Two bouncy bunnies
playing a game of it
the game was ended
when one fell in a pit.

One bouncy bunny
was very alone
he began to cry
so he bounced off home.

Joelle O'Neill (8)
St James' RC Primary School, Bromley

HARRY POTTER AND THE PHILOSOPHER'S STONE

Hogwarts is a School of Magic,
break the rules and the results could be tragic.
Dumbledore is the wizard in charge,
Hagrid the gamekeeper is an ogre, he's large!

Harry Potter, the hero, is just eleven,
he lives with nasty relatives, his parents are in Heaven.
Hogwarts saves Harry for most of the year
but holidays he has to go back here.

Voldemort is evil, he's killed many, it's true,
as a baby Harry defeated him and got a scar too,
Voldemort was left powerless, but he has a plan,
Harry tries to stop him whenever he can.

Professor Snape, potion master makes cauldrons bubble
He doesn't like Harry and gets him in trouble.
But with friends Hermione and Ron,
Harry is careful not to get picked on.

There are four houses which pupils are divided in,
Hufflepuff, Ravenclaw, Gryffindor, Slytherin,
with points awarded throughout the year to win a cup.
Quidditch is a game which helps the points go up.

Our heroes are in Gryffindor and by the end of the year
Gryffindors win, everyone gives a loud cheer.
Harry, Hermione, Ron use the skills they're taught,
Hogwarts is saved, they stopped Voldemort!

Daniel Brindley (11)
St James' RC Primary School, Bromley

MY DAY AT SCHOOL

I get to school in the morning
And I just can't stop yawning
I get my pencil out of my tray
Then I ask what we're doing today
Mathematics is first, I have to use a chart
But then it's my favourite subject
Art
Get paper, paint and brushes out
But soon it's time to scream and shout
It's play time.

Then we take off our gloves and hats
And wipe our feet on the dirty mats
We walk into the hall, each with a ball
Then we are told
'It's PE.'
My friend hates this, he's got a bad knee.

We're halfway through the day
Another time for us to play
It's lunchtime
The phone keeps on ringing
But can't be heard as the choir is singing.

We all go back to class and sit on our chairs
Then we are told by our teacher to get into pairs
It's time for DT

We work hard all afternoon and the time just flies past
Then we look at the clock, it's time to go at last.

It's home time!

Thomas Knight (10)
St James' RC Primary School, Bromley

OK MUM I WILL STOP IN A MINUTE

Got to think quick
Where shall I go?
Got to think quick
Fingers moving fast.

OK Mum I will stop in a minute

Here I am quick as a flash
Here I am mustn't crash.

OK Mum I will stop in a minute.

You will get sore eyes
Just like flies
You will get no dinner
You won't be a winner.

OK Mum I am coming.

Alex Dumbrell (10)
St James' RC Primary School, Bromley

DESTINATION DORADO

On the road to El Dorado,
Our young hero stumbled on,
Tired, simple, wounded, weary,
Living off a single lemon bon-bon!

He was full of determination,
But to reach his destination,
He had to cross the sea of storms,
Where a mythical monster roams.

The Hydra was guarding something special,
A city created of gold.
Our hero did not know what to do,
Some of that gold he so wanted to hold!

On the road to El Dorado,
Our young hero died upon
The nearest shore of El Dorado,
Death was his destiny.

Niall Slater (10)
St James' RC Primary School, Bromley

ANIMAL PARADE!

It is time for the animal parade,

All the preparations have been made,
Wild elephants wave their trunks,
Urgh, while that horrible smell is sprayed by the skunks,
The monkeys swing and shout ah, ah, ooh, ooh,
While you hear the sound of the glorious cuckoo,
Hare and tortoise go for a race,
While all the geese go on a wild goose chase,
The rattlesnake shakes his rattle
At the plodding farmyard cattle,
The big blue whale does an enormous squirt,
The snail goes flying and gets hurt,
The centipede walks around proudly,
While the werewolf howls loudly.
It's the animal parade!

Jack Hughes (11)
St James' RC Primary School, Bromley

THE TREASURE CHEST

To get to the treasure chest,
You have to travel far and wide,
To somewhere that is very well known,
But someone who is full of pride,
Will not be able to find this pleasure.

The quest for the treasure has now begun.
A modest boy of only ten,
Under the golden sun,
His only shelter, a fox's den,
To find this wonderful treasure.

He starts his quest through thick and thin,
He comes upon a forest big,
He wanders in and makes a din,
And goblins jump and do a jig,
Singing 'You'll never find your treasure!'

A noble knight of Camelot,
Comes and slays the ugly goblins,
And says 'I will take you to Shallot,
This is a place of Noblins,
Funny creatures that guard the pleasure.'

They ride through many towered Camelot
And shout 'We have killed the horrible goblins.'
They travel through the solid gold shallott,
And slay all the terrifying noblins
And find the treasure chest.

They open it and there they find
Lots of gold and riches.
They travel home very rich,
And live a life full of bliss.

Rebecca Powell (10)
St James' RC Primary School, Bromley

HIDDEN TREASURES

When we played in the forest
It was lots of fun.
When my brother found a map
A treasure map.

We didn't know at first
We all shouted hooray.
What a good start to
A new day.

And so we went to go
And find the treasure.
We went deep into the forest
And saw the mark on the ground.

We started to dig and dig
And there we found
The really big
Treasure chest.

There was lots of jewels
And golden tools.
There was lots of chains
And piles of money.

We tried to stuff it in our pockets
Then heard a scary sound.
We saw a giant wolf
With teeth as sharp as needles.

We ran away with all of the jewels
And treasure dropping out of our pockets.
We left the wolf behind
And made our way home.

Laura Lee (9)
St James' RC Primary School, Bromley

THE CREATURE IN THE SKY

Alone in the sky,
Nothing to do,
A cloud sweeps by,
It looks very blue.

It feels meaningless,
Being the sun's mirror in the sky.
The sun gets the best job,
But it wonders why.

It looks icy,
Glowing through a cloud,
Spooky, lonely,
To whine it's not allowed.

It is mysterious,
It needs a friend soon,
It looks so serious
For this creature is the moon.

Jenny Sharpe (11)
St James' RC Primary School, Bromley

LIFE

Life it's a funny thing,
With actors and dancers and people that sing.
We all know the world will never change into a square,
And we all know that life isn't fair.

My sister is really funny,
And my brother's nose is always runny.
My mum and dad are great people,
And their favourite sweet is toffee and treacle.

Now this poem has to come to an end,
But you never know what's coming round the bend.
There's one thing people can never forget,
Is the people they've seen and the people they've met.

Charlotte Morgan (10)
St James' RC Primary School, Bromley

THE HIDDEN TREASURE

I was once on a mission to find some gold,
And it could be sold.
I have a map that will take me far,
It's just too bad I don't have a car.

I walked through a massive frost,
I'm so glad I didn't get lost.
My feet were aching,
And my legs were breaking
How far to go.

I'm nearly there
My feet are bare.
This city is so rare,
I had to stare.

I unwrapped the map,
With my cap on my head.
How I wish I could go to bed.

I saw the gold,
I'm so glad it hadn't been sold.
The gold wasn't old,
I put the gold in my bag,
I had done what I was meant to do.

Katherine Lee (9)
St James' RC Primary School, Bromley

EARTH VOYAGING

The news adopted showing
an evil army growing.
For where it is there's no knowing
the cup of life is glowing.

Though one man was determined to
and nobody knew his name.
He fought for justice and for truth
to stop their cheating game.

He had to find the crypted cup
before the army do.
The fate of the world was in his hands
he mustn't lose his cool.

He faced the army two to one
he looked them in the eye
for them the man was just a pun
it was sure that he would die.

He walked on by
his heart was running
the evil army
were deadly cunning.

The battle started fiercely raging
through thick and thin it continued ageing.
The bold, great man just kept on slaying
from side to side the villains waning.

He grabbed the cup which he had found
he looked onto the solid ground
he saw a sign and read aloud
'Drink once for love and two for pounds.'

Ciaran O'Mahony (9)
St James' RC Primary School, Bromley

THE STRANGE TREASURE

In a desert people say,
That a magic treasure lay,
Among the sands far away.

Does this treasure really exist
'It really does' people persist.
'Among the sands far away.'

Then an adventurer found a map,
Which led to where the treasure sat.
Among the sands far away.

He started a journey long and hard,
And all he had to eat was lard.
Among the sands far away.

As he got nearer his destination
Still high was his determination,
Among the sands far away.

He said 'I can have all the pleasure'
When he found the magic treasure
Among the sands far away.

When he opened the treasure up,
All there was a magic drinking cup
Among the sands far away.

The man put it in a tower
Because he underestimated its power
Among the sands far away.

There it lays
Until this day
Among the sands far away.

Pippa Cawley (9)
St James' RC Primary School, Bromley

IN A FARAWAY LAND

In a faraway land lies a treasure
More golden than El Dorado itself.
But where is this land that sounds so grand?
The treasure of the sunken ships.

In a faraway land lies a treasure
A treasure that's waiting for me.
I'm on my way
I'll be there next day to find the golden treasure!

In a faraway land lies a treasure
I hope it's still waiting for me.
There floats a shark in the dark,
But the dark nor the shark will block me from the treasure!

At this land there's the treasure
Sparkling a bright colour gold.
After the mission I told all that I knew
The treasure of sunken ships.

Joseph Murray (9)
St James' RC Primary School, Bromley

THE POWERS

Far, far, far away there was treasure that lay,
Through the forest in the sea you will find a cave.
The cave lies in a volcano but mind it is thirty feet beneath the ground.
The three treasure magic powers invisibility, flying
And wishing have never been found.

The treasure powers you can't buy
And trust me I always tell the truth.
Not even the cleverest people could find the treasure powers
Many people have tried to find the treasure
But always came back with flowers.

One day two girls called Kym and Kay,
Set out to find the treasure.
They went through the forest and in the sea
They found the treasure and set back home for tea.

Charlotte Dickinson (9)
St James' RC Primary School, Bromley

THE HIDDEN MAP

Down in the jungle there was a hidden map
Over the hills and past the bats.
I went to the cave far past the waves
Where I saw a big fat cat.

The map was big, the map was round,
The map was hidden past the well.
I went to the sea far past the bees
Where I saw a really big bee.

I was really scared for such a bee
I met an ant who was also scared.
He said to me 'Where are you going in such a hurry?
I answered back with a clap.
He said to me 'Why did you clap?'
I didn't answer back because I saw a bat.

I ran away on a bay
when I got on a boat.
I travelled and travelled
and then I got there
with a fright.
I raced past the bay
until I got home.

James Sutch (9)
St James' RC Primary School, Bromley

THE CASE OF THE GOLDEN CLOTH

Three, two, one . . .
We're off.
Searching for the golden cloth.
As the two teams race
And leave behind their base.

Team A and Team B.
Running anywhere they can see.
Digging down under until they reach the sea.
But they can't be stopped,
As some horses clopped.

Team A in red,
Team B in green,
On a sailing boat as seen
The tide, high in,
The boats looking dim.

'Come on' the crowd cried,
But the two teams were getting tired.
The greens were sighing,
The red were whining,
But they would never give up.

The teams got off the boat,
And they nearly got chased by a goat.
Team A and Team B
Ahead of them they could see,
A sign that read *'The Golden Cloth'*

So then they pushed and shoved
Leaving Team A holding up *The Golden Cloth.*

Lucy Hobbs (10)
St James' RC Primary School, Bromley

UNDER THE SEA THERE IS TREASURE FOR ME!

I'm very excited,
I've heard a tale.
There is some treasure
To collect, I think I'll fail,
It's underwater that's all I know,
I'll take my boat
Even if luck's percentage is zero.

I'll dive in deep,
If there is no success
I'll weep and weep.
What is that? I see a shimmer,
And then I see a little glimmer.

I swim towards a little hope,
Is it what I think?
I am sure my answer is nope.
I'm getting closer right this second,
It is in a box
Is that what you reckon?
Now shall I open it?

Wow!
Look at the gold
And sapphires.
I really do admire
Shining through the water.
It sets my eyes on fire,
My dream has finally come!

Jacob Cleveland (9)
St James' RC Primary School, Bromley

THE HIDDEN TREASURE

I was once on a mission,
To find some gold.
The gold could be sold,
The gold's price was very high.
My family needed it so I decided to try.

I packed up some sandwiches,
Then I was ready to go.
I phoned for a taxi, it came oh so slow.
As I swam in the sea,
I felt so, so free.

I dived down to the bottom,
On the lookout for the gold.
I saw a chest, the one I'd been told,
My back was now aching,
From my big tanks that are shaking.

I got to the chest and dug down deep,
Then to see my prize, I pulled it.
I got out my key, it fit!
I swam up to the shore,
My family would love thee for sure.

As I got home my wife said out,
'Terry you're the best!'
Then made me a drink full of zest.
Suddenly my children cried out,
'We are rich!'

Cassie Cava (10)
St James' RC Primary School, Bromley

THE BATTLE FOR THE TREASURE

I sailed in the stormy weather
With the map as light as a feather.
The hidden treasure getting closer
The other team were gaining fast.
And at the moment we were last.
The hidden treasure getting closer.

I sailed onto some sandy land
And found myself very tanned.
The hidden treasure getting closer
I saw a big block of rock
And had a look at my clock.
The hidden treasure getting closer.

The block of rock split in two
And then I knew what I had to do.
The hidden treasure getting closer
I looked and saw a creaky door
And knocked it flat on the floor.
The hidden treasure getting closer.

I feasted my eyes on the treasure chest
And thought to myself I'm the best.
I've found the hidden treasure.
I grabbed the treasure
And sailed away with a lot of pleasure.
I've found the hidden treasure.

Daniel Hobbs (10)
St James' RC Primary School, Bromley

TREASURES OF THE MIDDLE EARTH

I have heard far away, on that day treasures lay,
Some red, some blue, some darker blue than you.
I know what to do, mustn't stay, got to make my way this day.
I'm going soon, very soon, going down the Earth's crust,
I must, must, must.

I know where the treasure is, but I just can't measure it,
It's a long way away, just another day to play.
The lava's red, the dragon's blue, all he does is play with you,
I know he's hard but he's a guard!

I'm there, I'm there, but it's just not fair,
The chest is open, there's nothing there except
A pear, a golden pear, a very special pear there lied.
As all those years pass and died.

My boss is cross, very cross,
Although he's happy in some way.
He'll have to wait another day.

John Griffin (10)
St James' RC Primary School, Bromley

THE WIND

The gale that passes by your face
As you walk along at a very slow pace.
You start to shiver, you are so weak,
You are so cold, you cannot speak.
And as you walk you start to pray
That tomorrow will be a warmer day.

Nina Smyth (11)
St James' RC Primary School, Bromley

OUT SHOPPING

We all walk to the shops.
The superstore is busy and all its shelves are stacked with goods.
The shopping is fun.
Mum gets her list.
I go and get the tea bags.
The boys choose the biscuits.
I ask if we can get some crisps.
Mum is looking at pizza and what to have for dinner.
The baby is asleep in the trolley.
We are going to buy bread and milk for breakfast in the mornings.
Now we are going to the checkout to pay.
We have to carry the shopping, it is heavy.
I hope we haven't forgotten the jelly.

Jodie Mackerill (8)
St Joseph's RC Primary School, Dartford

BEST FRIENDS

Would a best friend let you down?
Would a best friend take your last sweet?

Mine did!

Would a best friend take your bike away from you?
Would a best friend tell a secret on you?

Mine did!

'Sorry for letting you down
Sorry for taking your last sweet, you can have a pack.'

'I thought you were not friends with me.'

Mostafa Abdel-Kader (9)
St Joseph's RC Primary School, Dartford

MY FRIENDS

First there's Katrina,
She's a ballerina,
She spins and twirls
Just like all the other girls.
She has lots of golden curls
And wears a dress of pearls.

Next there's Pat,
She's an acrobat,
She spins and loops
Over bars and hoops
And to end the show
She'll wave and bow low.

Thirdly there's Amanda,
She has a pet salamander,
She jumps so high,
Wondering why
She can almost touch the sky!

Last but not least there's Kate,
She loves to skate,
She whizzes up and down the street,
In any weather, shine or sleet.
With a line so neat,
You wouldn't know it had been made by feet.

Ciara Smith & Sophie Kulczycki (10)
St Joseph's RC Primary School, Dartford

WINTERTIME IS NEAR

Wintertime is near,
Winter is in the air
Calm and peaceful as a deer
As Christmas is near.
Now the frost is here,
Everyone is in gear.
Slippery roads, cars and more,
But I am tucked up in bed
And I know so little
Because Christmas is near.
And as I wake to see the day,
The children are coming out to play.
Snow is here,
They all cheer
Winter is here.

Suzie Turrell (9)
St Joseph's RC Primary School, Dartford

DIFFERENT ANIMALS

Animals, animals everywhere!
in the world and in the air.
Some with spots and some with stripes,
some with fur and some with spikes.
Oh look I see a bear, brown and hairy
roaring hard
people screaming, running
jumping animals, animals everywhere.

Hannah Daniels (9)
St Joseph's RC Primary School, Dartford

IN THE DARK

It's nine o'clock, I'm in my bed,
Snuggled down with my ted.
I've been in bed an hour since,
I hear a noise that makes me wince.
A spider crawls across the wall,
His shadow makes him ten feet tall.
A small fieldmouse his whiskers quiver,
The thought of him makes me shiver.
I hear a bump upon the stair,
Is it a troll leaving its lair?
Someone's on the second floor,
I hear a creak from my bedroom door.
The shadows give way to the light,
My heart thuds quickly with the fright.
My mum bends down and strokes my head
She says 'Come on now it's time for bed.'

Lhiane Jenner (8)
St Joseph's RC Primary School, Dartford

GET WELL SOON

I hope you are OK,
I wonder how it went,
I haven't seen you all day,
So this is what I meant,
Get well soon.

I'm so glad you're home now,
I have really missed you too,
Can I see what was done? Wow,
But all I wanted to say to you,
Get well soon.

Andrea Regan (10)
St Joseph's RC Primary School, Dartford

ANIMAL HOUSE

I woke up one morning
And while I was yawning
I heard some growling
And then some howling
There was squawking
And lots of feet walking
I could hear the sound of claws
And the patter of many paws.

I scrambled out of bed
And poked my head round the door
I couldn't believe what I saw
Animals covered every inch of floor.

There was a bear in a chair
A racoon in the bath
A mink in the sink
And a hyena having a laugh.

A sheep was asleep in the spare room
A monkey cleaned up with a broom
A barn owl was perched on a towel
While a pig in a wig danced a jig.

I screamed 'Get out of my house!'
And pushed them out the door.
The last to go was a family of bears
Just when I thought they had all gone
I turned around and saw
There was a camel on the stairs!

Megan Smith (8)
St Joseph's RC Primary School, Dartford

A Witch's Kitchen

Opening a green and bashed door,
I see a black cat with beady eyes,
The black bent hat,
In the green door.

Jars with eyeballs inside,
Croaking toads jumping wildly,
A dusty old spellbook,
In the green door.

A snapped wand bent into shapes,
Cobwebs with hairy, black spiders in the middle of the web,
In the green door.

Rats scuffling around the floor,
A chair practically fallen apart,
In the green door.

Rebecca Farrell (9)
St Joseph's RC Primary School, Dartford

Seasons

In winter it is very dark,
With lots of snow in little sparks.

In spring it's a bit better
But best of all it's not wetter.

In summer the sun glimmers,
Flowers bloom and windows shimmer.

In autumn the weather is getting cold,
Leaves on trees turning gold.

Maria Bull (10)
St Joseph's RC Primary School, Dartford

A Winter's Day

Snowflakes drifting to the ground,
White clean snow all around.
Bare brown trees gently sway.
That's what starts a winter's day.

Children playing in the park
Getting colder, getting dark.
Having a last go on the sleigh.
That's what makes a winter's day.

Warm apple pie smells drift out,
Children running, start to shout.
'Come on, hurry up' they say.
That's what makes a winter's day.

Children going upstairs,
Adults going downstairs.
Saying goodnight,
Switching off the light.
That's the end of a winter's day.

Amy Leung (9)
St Joseph's RC Primary School, Dartford

Snowman

S now is white and cold,
N ow it is in winter, winter is cold.
O ver the fields we go playing all day.
W inter is the cold time, when we need hats and scarves.
M aking things to put on the Christmas tree.
A nd things to eat and drink.
N ow everyone goes to bed at night.

Rhiannon Bernard (8)
St Joseph's RC Primary School, Dartford

WHEN I GO TO BED

When I go to bed
I cuddle up with Ted,
He keeps me nice and warm
And keeps me safe from harm.

He makes me go to sleep
With his snoring little beat,
When I wake up in the morning
Little Ted is still yawning.

Rise and shine
Nearly out of time,
As I'm off for school
For nine.

I brush my teeth
And comb my hair,
Wait up Mum
I'm almost there.

Maria Wall (9)
St Joseph's RC Primary School, Dartford

ABOUT ME!

My mum says 'You must try harder'
I do the best I can!
But I really don't like reading
Just a bit of daydreaming.
'Perhaps you'd like to watch a video'
Now that's a different story!

Louise Nathanielsz (8)
St Joseph's RC Primary School, Dartford

A WITCH'S KITCHEN

I see a cauldron
And a spellbook
In the witch's kitchen.

I see a broomstick
And a rat
In the witch's kitchen.

I see cobwebs all around the kitchen
And a shabby looking wig
In the witch's kitchen.

I see a black witch's hat which at the top is pointy
I see a beady eyed cat
In the witch's kitchen.

I see some potions what are green and very small
I see a chair
In the witch's kitchen.

Jessica Moles (9)
St Joseph's RC Primary School, Dartford

WIND

Wind, wind,
Blow your trees down.
But please do not knock
My smile into a frown.
You can blow me away
You can turn me upside down
But please, please do not turn
My smile into a frown.

Kayleigh O'Connell (8)
St Joseph's RC Primary School, Dartford

BEING IN HOSPITAL

My room is filled with flowers
Books and games to pass the hours.

Lots of furry friends
To cheer me while my leg mends.

My own private nurse
The kindest in the universe.

Lots of food and sweets to eat
To help me get back on my feet.

A great TV and video screen
The likes of which I've never seen.

Lots of cards and photographs
To give me lots of smiles and laughs.

But mostly what I wish for more
Is to walk back through the school door.

Roisin Young (9)
St Joseph's RC Primary School, Dartford

INSIDE OF ME

Inside of me
I feel,
I feel,

Burp!

Free!

Nicola Seal (9)
St Joseph's RC Primary School, Dartford

A ROSE

A rose, a rose,
That sits in a vase
Blow wind, blow
But still the rose stands
Not breaking, or dying,
Just there in a vase.

The rose, the rose,
Stands there night and day
Just waiting for a friend
She looks and sees
Others with friends
But not her.

Jade Easton (9)
St Joseph's RC Primary School, Dartford

LUNCH

When I eat my lunch
Sometimes I eat it in a bunch
I eat my roll
And I think of my doll
I am cold
But is my cheese old?
And I eat my jelly
When it is too wobbly.
I put it in my welly
That is the end of my big, fat lunch.

Katrina Groves (8)
St Joseph's RC Primary School, Dartford

A Witch's Kitchen

Bubbly, green bogy potions lay on the sides.
Slimy, bloodshot eyeballs hang off the shelves.
Wooden broomsticks lay on the dusty, musty floor.
Grey, shabby, broken cobwebs lay everywhere.
That's how it is in a witch's kitchen.

Harriet Butler-Ellis (8)
St Joseph's RC Primary School, Dartford

The Tigers Run Free

The tigers run free in the wild,
they roar, they hunt, they play.
The crocodiles and alligators
hunt for their food
and the tigers hunt for their prey.

Tasha Young (9)
St Joseph's RC Primary School, Dartford

Colourful Me

My hair is blondish yellow
My eyes are browny green
My skin is sort of pinkish
My heart is very keen
All the colours I am inside
Have not yet been seen.

Natasha Hamilton-Brown (11)
Sevenoaks Prep School

HIDDEN TREASURES

Hidden treasure is not gold under sand
Or something you hold in the palm of your hand
Nor is it making someone mortified
Or knowing 29.99 pied.
Neither is it diamonds shiny and blue
Or laughing at someone who's less fortunate than you.
It isn't laughing when we beat Hilden Grange
Laughing and howling like we were deranged.
It isn't something you should hide
But something golden that glitters inside.
It doesn't glitter when you show off to your friends
It glitters when you try to make amends.
It doesn't matter how much you get
Or if you own a fighter jet.
The thing with which we should never part
Is the gold that glitters in our heart.

Winston Surrey (11)
Sevenoaks Prep School

THESE FEELINGS INSIDE

These feelings inside
They are so strange
I cannot describe
They stay within me
I can't be freed, I cannot thrive
Don't do it they say
They cannot die
Within my stomach bay
Inside me they fly
Crying hooray
These feelings inside.

Steen Tranholm Reed (10)
Sevenoaks Prep School

THE NEW BOY

There he is in the corner, on his own,
Putting all his stuff into the desk,
He is very nervous as the teacher hands him his books,
The class wonders:
What is his name? Where does he come from?
Does he like Arsenal? Is he good at football?

We go to our first lesson.
He sits in the corner again.
He is not writing any answers down,
Yet he is too scared to ask the teacher.
The teacher tries to be friendly,
But he doesn't even smile.

At break time he gets his Break out
And slowly eats it in the corner,
Trying to waste time.
But he finishes it early.
All the boys say,
'Do you want to play football?'
He says no.

At the end of break when everyone comes in,
He is still in the classroom,
Sorting out his books and naming his pencil cases.
Someone offers to sit next to him,
He declines.

I wake up.
It was just a dream.
My mum is telling me to get up for my big day.
I suddenly remember.
I start at my new school today.
That boy was me!

William Ritchie (11)
Sevenoaks Prep School

HIDDEN TREASURE

There's hidden treasure everywhere,
You'll just have to look, though you don't know where.
It could be here, it could be there,
There's hidden treasure everywhere.

It could be hidden in the sea,
Underground or in a tree.
It's waiting to be found by you or me,
It could be there for eternity.

You may pass it every day,
'Look at that rubbish' is what you may say.
Be careful before you give it away,
It might be worth a lot some day.

Just keep looking, it could be rare,
It could be in the attic or under the stair.
So next time you're bored, don't just sit there,
Because there's hidden treasure everywhere.

Mike Higgs (11)
Sevenoaks Prep School

I AM COOL SO I MUST RULE THE SCHOOL

I am cool so I must rule the school,
not Miss Ball she makes us do press-ups in the hall,
not Mrs Chair she has too much hair, not me though,
I am cool so I must rule the school.

Not Mr Shield he makes us run around the field,
not Danny Rust he makes us clean up the dust,
but I wouldn't do any of that because I am
cool so I must rule the school.

Mark Lucas (10)
Sevenoaks Prep School

SNOWMAN

My snowman is cute and white
In his mouth he has a pipe
Down his chest he has his buttons
On his stick arms he has his mittens.

I put upon his head and on his stick arms
A woolly hat in red and mittens on his palms.

I love my sweet snowman
Everyone else is a no-man
First beauty prize he would have won
But now he has melted away and
Gone.

Raffaella Buck (10)
Sevenoaks Prep School

VISITING FROM GERMANY

It's not Potter's Hermione,
But my auntie Monster.
Mornings she won't stare,
Seeing the owls flying.
Evenings she will hear bats crying.
In the night she will push clouds,
And without any doubts,
No rain will be falling.
All family is calling:
'Make our house really bright,
All day and all night!'

Paul Boles (11)
Sevenoaks Prep School

MY PONY

My pony shiny and black
will canter through fields and meadows.
I ride her on the moor
where we meet all types of horses,
all of different colour.
Horses have always been useful to man.
Like in war where they have charged for man'
honour and pride through fire of other man.
My pony would charge but I wouldn't let her
if it was up to me.
But alas it would be up to England and the Empire.
Horses have used their muscles for men,
like pull ploughs and coaches for man, food and transport.
I wouldn't let my pony charge if it was up to me,
but alas it's not.

Ben Regan (10)
Sevenoaks Prep School

WHAT A PUPPY MIGHT DO ALL DAY

I'm a little puppy chasing that bad cat Fluffy
I guard the house from ten-past one till half-past four.

My owner is very nice but definitely not poor.
Then we go to the park and play a game of catch.
After that we go and watch the cricket match just down the road.
Then off we go home.

But don't forget I'm just a puppy and I do not like that cat Fluffy,
but definitely like playing catch and watching the cricket match.
Just down the road.

Charlotte Smith (11)
Sevenoaks Prep School

AUTUMN

Autumn, summer over, winter coming.
Birds migrating
Grass, no longer growing.
Animals hibernating.

Evergreens never dropping their leaves
Sunny days, cold, clear blue sky.
Cold, cold wind, snow ahead
Waterlogged gardens, or crisp and dry.

Guy Fawkes burning,
Bonfire blazing,
Sausages sizzling,
Potatoes baking.

Hot chocolate steaming,
Marshmallows toasting.
Mulled wine brewing,
Chestnuts roasting.

Harriet Partridge (10)
Sevenoaks Prep School

IF I WAS AN ANIMAL . . .

I'd be a monkey in the jungle
all day swinging from tree to tree.
No care for what's on the ground
beneath me.
There's no other animal I'd rather be
The monkey life is the way for me.
I'd talk with friends 'ahh ahee ee'
And all day playing in the tree.
I wish I was a monkey.

Jonny Drown (11)
Sevenoaks Prep School

PITCH-BLACK

I went for a stroll in the dark
The wind was whistling
And the owls were hooting.
Then I heard some shooting
It was getting darker.
The moon was out,
Without a doubt.
I was getting scared.
Then I heard someone coming.
I was panicking, the sound was getting closer,
I heard leaves crunching on the grass from footsteps.
It was getting louder.
I saw something move over there!
There he was!
I thought I should try and find my way back,
But I couldn't because it was
Pitch-black!

Anthony Kayne (10)
Sevenoaks Prep School

MY BABY BROTHER

My baby brother is really cuddly,
His cheeks are soft and really snuggly.

His hair is ginger and really shiny,
This little boy is called Tivey

He is very small and very sweet,
He has also got very big feet.

He laughs and he cries and he poos his nappy,
Apart from that he's very happy.

Tarra Nichols (11)
Sevenoaks Prep School

THE COUNTRY

The country is a wonderful place,
Wildlife, farms anything you name.
There's no mud to get on your face.

The country is a terrible place,
Rats, bombs, industrial landfill.
They compete for the land, it's a *race!*

Two places, one light, one black
Live in the nice one get on the right train.
One paradise but one is death!

Aim for the bright place
With the sun on your face.
Stay away from death
Or you will die of Drainatonga.

William Harris (11)
Sevenoaks Prep School

EXTRA BODY PARTS

Imagine you were born with three extra hands!
And here and there some extra legs.
With fingers eleven,
Or pairs of eyes seven,
With some toes nine
Set out in a line.
With two sets of ears on each side
And a super long tongue extra wide,
With two extra arms and two extra jaws
And instead of hands you would have paws.
I feel sorry if you were
Cos with others it doesn't occur.

Vincent Post (11)
Sevenoaks Prep School

UNTITLED

There was a young dude from Dubai
Who let out a very big cry
With another big cry he felt so shy
And wished he could fly away.

With a breath of air
He thought he would share
A silence to his delight.
To his fright he saw a kite land on his sore red eyes.

To his sight
He saw a light
Coming from a boy
The little boy was not shy.

To his delight
He saw a sight that gave him a terrible fright.
A man was standing beside him.
He decided to be polite not exposing his fright.

He rode upon his bike
And took his fright
As the light came closer
His fright began to die.

Andrew McDowall (9)
Sevenoaks Prep School

EYES IN THE DARK

Traipsing through the dingy wood
Darkness closing in,
Broken twigs and branches lay
Beneath my raw, bare skin.

I stop to find a rustling
To my left and right.
I walk a little further on,
Still petrified with fright.

Something darts in front of me,
I yell and scramble back.
Two blinking green eyes stare at me
Then vanish with a snap!

Hours later I reached my goal
And found that I was back,
I thought I'd seen those eyes before,
'Twas Nigel, my tabby cat!

Amy Salt (11)
Sevenoaks Prep School

TEACHERS

Teachers are so very boring,
Never working, always snoring.
They always are so very smug,
When sipping from their cocoa mug.
They always make us do loads of work,
In fact, they treat us lower than dirt.
In break they sit in their grotty little lounge,
While we make good use of our football ground.

They have the most old-fashioned cars,
Like Mini Metros and 1940 Jaguars.
Teachers are my worst nightmare,
They're something I just can't bear.
In fact, practically,
We should order some fresh teachers from the factory.
But fortunately none of this is true,
Unless the teacher I'm talking about is
          You!

Edward Cloke (10)
Sevenoaks Prep School

DIRTBIKES

The engines are growling
The drivers are poised
On your marks, get set, go!

Wheels spinning, churning out mud
Over the jump, down with a thud.

Lean to the left, lean to the right
It's going to be extremely tight.

As we go round the corner
Into the home straight
The pressure is mounting.

The other riders are closing in
The heat is on
The finish line is dead ahead.

I'm skidding out of control now
Kaboom, bang, screech ow!

Kassim Ramji (10)
Sevenoaks Prep School

THE STRAY

I was walking one day when I came across a stray.
I thought to myself poor stray all ugly and grey.
Its hair was tangled,
Knotted and mangled,
It was covered in flees,
As skinny as could be.
I felt sorry for that stray,
But what could I do?
So I left him, then came back at noon,
And there I stood on my own,
But I wasn't absolutely alone,
For there before me was the stray,
His hair still matted, that ugly grey.
So I left him alone,
For I couldn't take him home.
Then I returned the next day,
And that's where he'll stay,
Still ugly and grey.
Oh that poor, poor stray,
I wish I could take him away.

Kathryn Dendias (11)
Sevenoaks Prep School

DOGS

Dogs are big,
Dogs are small,
Dogs are short
And dogs are tall.

They bark and bark,
They eat and eat,
They love to walk
And lick your feet.

But they're the best,
They're man's best friend,
They'll always be there
In the end.

That's why I love them,
I really do,
They're my best pet
And I have two.

Zoe Montanaro (11)
Sevenoaks Prep School

BEAUTIFUL CREATURES OF THE SEA

Swim beautiful creatures
For the fishermen are reaching.

Ships are bobbing
And so are you.

Crabs are munching
And gulls are swooping.

Dolphins are leaping
And nets are catching.

Waves are splashing
Sea horses are gliding.

Fishes of all colours
Are in hiding.

Tide calm down
Midnight is all around.

Swim beautiful creatures
For the fishermen are leaving.

Alice Bramall (10)
Sevenoaks Prep School

CARS

Cars go broom
Cars go zoom
Just like the va va voom
Ford is the lord
Jag is no fag
Rolls Royce doesn't get bored
Bentley is not a drag
Mini is no weenie
Lotus is not atrocious
Cars go broom
Cars go zoom
Just like the va va voom.

Michael Tynan (10)
Sevenoaks Prep School

THE MOON

The moon dazzles
like a light bulb in a pumpkin.
The moon twinkles
like a star in the sky.
The moon blazes
like a flame of fire.
The moon shines
like a disco ball in a party.
The moon sparkles
like a flash of light.

Jason Carver (9)
Sussex Road CP School

THE MOON

Glitters
like a giant pile of silver coins
Flickers
like a new RAF badge
Glistens
like a shiny cup that's just been won in a swimming club
Sparkles
like some twinkling dots in the pitch-black sky
Gleams
like a silver pond in an open field
Glints
like a giant, new five pound coin in the sky shining.

Joshua Lincoln (9)
Sussex Road CP School

THE MOON POEM

The moon gleams
like a star shining up in the sky.
The moon is big like a ball.
There is a man living in the moon,
he has black hair.
He is reading a Harry Potter book.
A star is twinkling in the sky.
The moon is bright
like a light.
The moon is far away.

Amy Munday (9)
Sussex Road CP School

THE MOON

Glows
like a torch hanging from the dark roof.
Glitters
like a diamond in a high up museum.
Gleams
like pearls on a dark black piece of paper.
Sparkles
like a white gem in a dark box.
Twinkles
like a star in the sooty sky.
Glistens
like a gold ring in the gloomy night.

Jonathan Nazer (8)
Sussex Road CP School

THE MOON

Glows
like a magic sticker stuck on a black piece of paper.
Twinkles
like a giant twinkling star living in different dark tunnels.
Sparkles
like a disco ball hanging from a black ceiling.
Glitters
like a white pen waiting to be used on a black piece of card.
Gleams
like a special diamond showing the way through a pitch-black mine.
Glistens
like a gold ring shining on a black cushion.

Samuel Truscott (8)
Sussex Road CP School

THE MOON

Glitters
like a disco ball hanging from the dark sky above.
Twinkles
like a metal buckle on my shoe in a dark cupboard.
Glistens
like a metal pencil case under a desk spotlight
in a room as dark as a cellar.
Glows
like a diamond in an old dark school off a teacher's necklace.
Shimmers
like a precious diamond under the ground.
Shines
like a lady's eye.

Nicola Drew (8)
Sussex Road CP School

THE MOON

The moon glows
like a 10p coin dropped into a deep well.
Sparkles
like silver tinsel on an evergreen tree.
Glistens
like a pair of earrings in a velvet bag.
Gleams
like a blazing fire in a blackened fireplace.

Andrea Sargent (9)
Sussex Road CP School

THE MOON

Gleams
like a misty crystal ball in a magician's cave.
Glimmers
like a shiny copper coin in a dark pocket.
Glints
like a gold ring in a jeweller's shop.
Twinkles
like a glowing light in the distance of a night-time parade.
Sparkles
like an exploding firework set off for Bonfire Night.
Glows
like a red-hot fire to be used for a magical spell.

Lauren Rickard
Sussex Road CP School

THE MOON

Gleams
like a crystal ball hanging over the dance floor.
Glimmers
like a silver mirror on a stone wall.
Glows
like a milky pearl on a piece of black velvet.
Shines
like a round clock face in the classroom at night.
Sparkles
like coloured sequins on a dark cushion.
Twinkles
like a precious diamond in a deep box.

Emma Gilham (9)
Sussex Road CP School

THE MOON

The moon twinkles
like tinsel on an evergreen Christmas tree.

The moon glows
like a red-hot fire all around Guy Fawkes on Firework Night.

The moon glimmers
like a new coin dropped down a deep drain.

The moon gleams
like a diamond waiting to be bought in a jewellers.

The moon glistens
like a diamond ring twinkling in the distance.

The moon sparkles
like a firework shooting up to the sky.

Nicole Standage
Sussex Road CP School

THE MOON

The moon sparkles like a sheet in your bed
It shines like a shiny diamond case
It gleams like an eye in a tree
It looks as big and silver as an owl
It glistens like a silver can
It's like a silver case
It gleams like an owl in a tree
It sparkles like a new shiny ring with some gold.

Ben Woods (9)
Sussex Road CP School

THE MOON

Sparkles
it shines like a star.
Flashes
lovely night bulb, it flashes like a king.
Sparkles
silver can.
Shimmers
dimmed lemon shape.
Gleams
cheerless-shaped moon.
Shines
gleaming moon.

Robert Jackson (8)
Sussex Road CP School

THE MOON

Sparkles
like a bright light in the cellar.
Glows
like a torch in a cave.
Twinkles
like a shiny star.
Gleams
like a gold medal.
Shines
like a coin in a well.
It dazzles
like a spit of fire.

Adam Hammond (9)
Sussex Road CP School

THE MOON

Sparkles
like a gleaming tooth just fallen out.
Twinkles
like a dazzling light in the sky.
Gleams
like a lamp in a dark room.
Flares
like a shiny diamond waiting to be dug out of the ground.
Dazzles
like an unwanted light bulb in the dump.
Glistens
like a milky pearl in the sea.

Tyler Dunlop
Sussex Road CP School

THE MOON

The moon gleams
like a silver medal on the chest of an athlete.
Dazzles
like a piece of water out of a hose.
Glimmers
like a shining sapphire in a museum's case.
Blazes
like a magnifying glass in a desert.
Glistens
like a circular white book cover.
Glows
like a shiny sticker in the dark.

Robert Fenwick (9)
Sussex Road CP School

THE MOON

The moon shines gracefully
like it is hanging like a big magic ball of spells.
Brightly gleams in the sky
like a calm pearl in the sea that caught your eye.
Beams up high like a stone with a face in it.
Shines in the sky like a crystal ball.
Gleams the stars like a ball going too fast.

Sophie Warnett (9)
Sussex Road CP School

THE MOON

Glows
like a magic sticker in a dark room.
Glitters
like a disco ball hanging from a pitch-black ceiling.
Flickers
like a milky pearl on a sooty black dress.

Luke Webber (9)
Sussex Road CP School

THE MOON

The moon glows
like a postman's jacket in the dark.
The moon gleams
like a shooting star so high in the sky.

The moon shines
like a headlight on a car, it's so bright.
The moon sparkles
like a Catherine wheel.

Luke Chatfield (9)
Sussex Road CP School

THE MOON

The moon shines like a rough diamond in a deep mine.
The moon glistens like a one pound coin that just came out of a mint.
The moon dazzles like a bright light from the sun.
The moon sparkles like a body of ice at the Battle of Hastings.
The moon twinkles like water from a bubbler.
The moon glints like a piece of steel on London Bridge.

Matthew Rutch (9)
Sussex Road CP School

THE MOON

The moon shines like a massive star
The moon blazes like a bright light
The moon glows like a big ball
The moon glistens like a big, glistening rocket
The moon sparkles like a piece of cold ice
The moon glitters like a glittering pearl.

Jamie Curtis-Jones (8)
Sussex Road CP School

DAY BY DAY

My name is Lauren and I'm a girl,
I've got leukaemia with a story to tell.
Back in July I found bruises and more . . .
I felt really tired and my gums became sore.
So off to the dentist who filled in my tooth,
And now I'm in here my '2x4' booth.
This booth is my room, on Farnborough's Hayes Ward
Where they give me my Chemo that made me go bald.
The treatment is horrid and makes me feel sick
Please tell me why this cancer chose me to pick!
I get really angry, hurt and feel sad
And even get nasty, spiteful and mad.
Why choose me, am I really that bad?
My brother and sister are the ones who are loud.
I've always been good and said my 'Ps & Qs'
But that wasn't enough, and now I have the blues.
It's not always bad and sometimes even good
Cos now I don't have to eat the greens that I should.

I miss going to school, especially my friends,
The playing around and swapping of pens.
I've really grown up in these last few months
The road has been filled with hurdles and bumps.

All I can do is hope this leukaemia goes away
But until then, I will take things day by day.

One year has passed, and I am well.
So part two of my story, I will try to tell.
A lot has happened in the last twelve months,
My journey has been filled with hurdles and bumps.

I am back at school and playing with friends.
Not much as changed, we still swap gel pens.
I missed lots of school, so I have to catch up,
And all of my friends say that's just bad luck.

The homework is easy, not like *All*
so I am lucky to be here with my story to tell.
I am used to my illness, it is not a big deal
I still get scared because leukaemia can kill.

Sometimes I get frightened, and think my illness won't go.
The thought of doing it all again, makes me feel low.

I have to be strong, and keep a clear head,
And remember a year ago I was too ill to get out of bed.

I have been through a lot but so have we all,
My brother and sister have been really cool.

Maggie my nurse, told me it won't always be bad,
She told me the truth, and for this, I am glad.

Everyone has been great and I want to say thank you
Especially the nurses for all that they do.

Lauren Knight (10)
Southborough Primary School

DASH CAT

Through the house I like to dash
upstairs, downstairs in a flash.
Don't get anything in my way,
or I might stop to have a play.
Eventually I'll have a rest,
Then I'm cute and not a pest.
Wake up time and off I go
Dashing quickly around not slow.
Don't put your feet out to make me stop,
A sore toe will be what you've got.

Sarah Bristow (8)
Southborough Primary School

THE THING

It's big and hairy,
No it's not a fairy,
It has a big bushy tail,
And no it's not male!

She's black and tan,
And sometimes I'm a fan,
She's very, very silly,
But her name's not Billy!

She has big, hairy paws,
And very sharp claws,
She's always in the way,
And never listens to a word I say!

She's not exactly a bright spark,
And her heart's definitely not dark.
Have you guessed what it is yet?
It's my pet!

Sadie.

Laura Blackman (10)
Southborough Primary School

THE BIG FAT CAT

The cat, the cat, the big fat cat
Who sat, who sat, who sat on the on the mat.
The cat, the cat, the big fat cat
Went to the door and went rat-a-tat-tat.
The big fat cat saw a rat and named the
Little rat a lovely name called Pat.
A bat saw Pat and the big fat cat
And was jealous of Pat and the cat.

So the bat went to Pat and the cat
And the bat said 'Hello fat cat.
Oh hello small rat
My name is Bat.'
'My name is Pat and this is
My friend fat cat.'
And they were all best pals.

Bat, Pat and last of all the big fat cat.

Wemimo Onashoga (9)
Southborough Primary School

BIG SISTER, LITTLE SISTER

I'm a little sister
being bossed around
by my big sister.

All my sister does
is be rude to me.

I have to share a room with her
she keeps me up at night
and she always ignores me
in getting so fed up.

Why can't she be kind to me?
I've seen her do it before then.
Trust me you don't want a big sister!

Samantha Martin (8)
Southborough Primary School

LOVE

Love can be fun
Love can be cool
Love can be better than having
A swimming pool.

Love is love
Like a dove
Flying in the air
As a hairy bear.

I can love you
And you can love me
As long as we're together
In perfect harmony.

Paige Sutherland & Amy Kither (10)
The Brent CP School

DOG

Long walker
Ball chaser
Biscuit cruncher
Lip drooler
Tail wagger
Bone burier
Good fetcher
Meat eater
Heavy puffer
Big biter
Body guarder
Slimy licker
Water drinker.

Donna Constant (11)
The Brent CP School

DOG

Bottom sniffer
Bone burier
Fast eater
Wet nose
Man's best friend
Door scratcher
Show off
Good hunter
Cat chaser
Football player
Shoe ripper
Loud barker
Lip drooler
Runaway!

Harrison Roberts (10)
The Brent CP School

MY KENNING

Wet licker
Bone burier
Good beggar
Bottom sniffer
Frisbee catcher
Cat chaser
Leg lifter
Ball attacker
Shoe ripper
Fence jumper
Sharp biter
Meat eater
Loud growler.

Daniel Jervis (11)
The Brent CP School

DANIELLA'S INSTRUCTIONS FOR GIANTS

Please do not step on me,
Burger King, old people's homes or sweet shops.
Please flatten all schools!

Please do not eat me,
Hear'say, money or animals.
Please feel free to gobble up clowns that are not
funny anytime you like!

Please do not block the sunshine!
Please push the wind and rain to Africa!

Please do not drink the rain!
Please eat all vegetables on Earth!

Daniella Diaz-Bates (10)
The Brent CP School

MY SPELL

Roundabout the cauldron go
In the beak of parrot throw,
and mad dog's bone and horse's heart,
a rotting bone.
For a spell of powerful trouble in the cauldron
boil and bubble stomach of human and ear scraped
up from a moulding body.
Bucket of fleas and green cheese
make charm to make zombies.

My magic potion would be for never coming to school.

Craig Wiltshire (11)
The Brent CP School

JENNY'S SPELL!

Roundabout the cauldron go;
Dead craneflies wings in they go;
Spiders legs and all those things,
Crushed fairies and all their wings.
Dead man's toe and all his nails,
A dragon's claw as big as a whale.
School dinners so slimy and bad,
A teacher's tongue so very mad.

My spell is for making your dreams come true.

Jenny Haines (11)
The Brent CP School

CHOCOLATE

I like chocolate, it's very nice,
It's a lot better than Indian rice.
I like chocolate very much,
So does my rabbit in its hutch.
Chocolate is the best thing in the world,
Sometimes flat and sometimes curled.

Carrie-Ann Shine (10)
The Brent CP School

FRIENDS

Friends you can trust
and they're not always in a rush.
They have time for your feelings
and when they are cut you help it to stop bleeding.
Friends are friends forever to trust.

Kiran Khattra (10)
The Brent CP School

PIGGY RHYME

I saw a pig in my garden green,
It was the funniest pig I'd seen.
The pig had wings
I asked him 'Why
Don't humans fly?'
The pig wanted to end the rhyme.
He said 'Maybe you could try this time.'

Rachel Pooley (10)
The Brent CP School

HAPPINESS

Happiness is sun yellow.
It tastes like Sunny Delight
And smells like extra spicy southern fried
Chicken nuggets.
It looks like a sun,
And sounds like a gentle breeze.
Happiness is really, really fun.

Daniel Russell (10)
The Brent CP School

ANGER

Anger is a very dark red.
It tastes like acid in the back of your throat,
and smells like a great burning fire.
Anger looks like someone is just about to explode,
and sounds like a kettle steaming.
Anger is like a raging volcano.

William Moore (10)
The Brent CP School

THE FRIENDLY DOG

The friendly dog ran into the dark
then he started to bark.
He saw some children having fun
and wanted to join the fun.
He bounced about and started to run
and chased the children for the ball
and landed against the wall.

Karen Smith (10)
The Brent CP School

HAPPINESS

Happiness is pink.
Happiness tastes like summer fruit.
Happiness smells like a summer fragrance.
Happiness looks like a sunny beach.
Happiness sounds like birds singing.
Happiness feels like a cool breeze.

Samantha Railton (9)
The Brent CP School

SADNESS

Sadness is a night blue,
Sadness tastes like salty water.
It smells like burnt paper,
And looks like a choppy sea.
It sounds like someone crying.
Sadness feels like rough sandpaper.

Nicholas Mills (10)
The Brent CP School

THE WITCH'S SPELL

Roundabout the cauldron go;
Deadly rabbits in they go,
A baby heart goes in too,
A mouldy sausage from the loo,
A mouldy eyeball you bet,
Rats tails will make the spell work.

My spell is for going into movies and cartoons!

Holly Ingram (10)
The Brent CP School

HAPPINESS

Happiness is a light blue.
It tastes like a fry up on a Saturday morning,
and it smells like fresh cookies.
Happiness looks like a bright blue sky,
and sounds like birds chirping away.
Happiness is a beach in a hot country.

Broden Ajgarni (10)
The Brent CP School

FEAR

Fear is red.
It tastes like blood
And smells like smoke.
Fear looks like a black shadow
And sounds like a train crashing towards you.
Fear is a shark trying to bite you!

Daniel Phillips (10)
The Brent CP School

SADNESS

Sadness is black,
It tastes like the salty sea
And smells like cheese and onion crisps.
It looks like a dead flower
And sounds like a slow song that goes on forever.
It feels like an imaginary world that you can't get out of.

Laura Ross (11)
The Brent CP School

HAPPINESS

Happiness is a shiny yellow,
It tastes like the best sweets,
It smells like a newborn kitten,
It looks like the sun bursting out through the rain,
It sounds like birds singing in your house
And it feels like a dog licking your face.

Tommy Hutchinson (10)
The Brent CP School

ANGER

Anger is raging hot red,
It tastes like red-hot chillies,
It smells like smoke from a burning hot fire,
Anger looks like the edge of the Earth,
Anger sounds like a devil's laugh,
It feels like Hell.

Toby Santinella (10)
The Brent CP School

HAPPINESS

Happiness is blue
It tastes like bubblegum
And smells like bluebells.
It looks like the sky on a sunny day
And sounds like bluebottles flying around.
It's brilliant.

Lucy Grant (10)
The Brent CP School

CALM

Calm is light green.
It tastes like a cold pudding,
and smells like the sea.
Calm looks like ice melting,
and sounds like the wind blowing.
Calm is fur off an animal.

Jaz Key (11)
The Brent CP School

THE WIND

The wind is like - like - hmm . . .

A strong wave at sea
A swift tiger chasing through the jungle
An imaginary cheetah pushing you around
An eagle - free, swooping in the air
A busy train station, everybody rushing around.
The wind is like a waterfall crashing at the rocks.

Laura Asplin (9)
Weald CP School

WOLF

The frost sparkled beneath his padded paws,
He was the midnight hunter,
On the prowl,
Howling at the moon,
He was alone,
Competing against nature,
He alone heard the owl,
And foraged for its nest,
A rustling in the bushes
Made his hackles rise,
His hair stood on end,
He drew back his lips to show his teeth,
Out of the bushes rose a great bear,
The air filled with snarls,
The wolf howled once,
And fled.
He fled to the moors,
Soft and slippery,
There the hunt began,
A roe deer,
Red, timid and gentle,
Prancing on the horizon,
Shadowed by the moon,
Not much bigger than he,
It fled on.
The wolf on its trail,
At last the deer stopped,
Caught in the quagmire,
The wolf pounced,
Fixed his teeth around her neck,
And feasted on her flesh.

Thomas Cochrane-Powell (9)
Weald CP School

PLEASE

'Mum can I have some sweets?'
'No! You eat too many!'
'OK can I have some crisps? Please.'
'No!'
'But!'
'But what? Your dinner will be ready soon!'
'That's too long, please, please, *please!*'

'Mum!'
'What now you pest?'
'Can I have a bike for my birthday?'
'No way! You've got a perfectly good bike in the shed! No buts go away!'
'Alright OK!'

'Mum!'
'Yes.'
'Do I have to go to school cos I don't want to?'
'Of course you do, don't be silly, go away.'
'But!'
'No buts.'

'Mum!'
'Yes!'
'Can I have a piece of fruit?'
'No!'
'What did you say?'
'Can I have some fruit?'
'Yeah, sure.'

Charlotte Vile (11)
Weald CP School

THE WART ON MY NOSE

Good grief this wart on my nose,
I squeezed it so much that I scrunched up my toes.
I put on a plaster,
I put on some cream,
I tried to prick it with a needle,
which just made me scream.
I can't blow my nose now,
'cause my nose really hurts,
So I made some bandages out of
my mum's old skirts.
We decided to go to the doctors,
to have this wart removed.
But when the doctor was approaching me,
I screamed and he got sued.
So we went down to Grandma's to see what she could do.
But when Grandma looked at it, she didn't have a clue.
It was getting dark by then,
So we decided to go home,
and by the time we got there,
we had ten messages on the phone.
I couldn't get to sleep that night,
'cause the pain on my nose was quite dire,
as my wart was burning and my nose was on fire.
In the morning I started to scream,
I wondered if it was real or was it my dream?
Well, my wart started growing all big and fat,
until it was big enough to go
splat!

Emily Kerr (10)
Weald CP School

THE MASSIVE FIREWORK

Fireworks!
Best thing that could happen at night.
They're like a big bolt of lightning.
A giant cracker about to pop . . . um . . .
Bang . . . Crash . . . Wallop . . .
Fireworks blast here and there
There even might be a um . . .

A big crash with two fireworks and . . .
Boom! A bang of wonderful colours to light up
all of the night.
Also . . . you would have to invent the *best*
fireworks ever, with a . . . colourful spark that
would light all of the night with a flash of sparkling light.

Suzanne Howe (9)
Weald CP School

THE SEA

From here the sea stretches as far as the horizon.
It's like a large wobbly jelly
That slips off the spoon like the rippling waves
But it changes so suddenly like a dancing flame
Waiting for more logs to make it roar
Washing seaweed on to the bay,
And the waves are like - like hmm . . .

Green bananas arranged like the foaming waves
Like abandoned material, scrunched up in a bag
Like a bike going fast through a puddle
And the jets from a spa spraying
Waiting to be turned off.

Charlotte Jarvis (9)
Weald CP School

THE SEA

The sea is like a big blue blanket,
Swept over the land.
Like a big wobbly jelly
Splashed on your plate.
Sometimes crashing against the rocks
Maybe silent like a *cold* winter night.
It's blue like . . .
Like an icy December morning,
Frost on the windows,
The back of jumping dolphins
And squirting whales.
A brand new metallic pen
Shining on the paper.
When the clock strikes midnight
and the night is
Dark.

Bridget Miller (9)
Weald CP School

THE SUN

Umm, the sun is like
A big ball of boiling lava
That's been pushed out of an erupting volcano.
A round ball of orange
And red sparks flying off a great bonfire.
An orange bowling ball
That's just been thrown.
A big yellow balloon that's
Floated into the sky
And stayed there forever.

Hannah Goozee (8)
Weald CP School

THE HAIRY THING

The hairy thing ran quickly through the snow,
With a great glow.
It knocked down every tree,
With glee.

The hairy thing ran quickly through the snow,
With a great glow,
It crashed down the buildings,
And stole all the gold rings.

The hairy thing ran quickly through the snow,
With a great glow.
Fixing everything he had done,
Then went off home.

Robert Cooper (10)
Weald CP School

THE FIREWORKS

Fireworks are the best
They are the shooting stars
In the midnight sky
Boom! Boom! They hang in the sky
Like a hunter shooting birds.

When they go into the sky
They make a splash of paint
Just been thrown onto a dark piece
Of paper
When it goes *boom!* it is like *glitter*
Oh how I love fireworks.

Samantha Holloway (9)
Weald CP School

MY MUM ON MONDAY

My mum on Monday,
first jumps up and down,
Then she jumps on the banister,
and slid down to the town.
She'll do her shopping,
dropping and breaking all the food.
Then she'll strip down into the
   Nude!
   How rude!
She'll dance round all the lamp posts.
She'll go in a food shop and eat all the toast.
She'll do the Full Monty in Victoria Hall.
She'll jump into Tonbridge swimming pool.
What an embarrassment!

Lucy Hall (10)
Weald CP School

THE NEW SCHOOL HEAD TEACHER

At school we have a new head teacher,
We have only had her for a week,
She's really, really mad,
And she thinks that we're all so very bad.
Her office is a rubbish heap,
She keeps a very woolly sheep.
Her rules are the strictest on this planet,
They're even more stricter than Mrs Janet.
Steam comes out of her ears.
She's drunk from too many beers,
And at the end of school she really, really grows.

Heather Olley (10)
Weald CP School

THINK

Why, why, why, oh why,
Why can't I fly?
Why can't I ever touch the sky?
This world is never down to Earth,
So many things to ask.
So why?

Why, why, why, oh why,
Why don't wars become peace?
Why do people never think of others?
They keep everything to themselves,
So many things to think.
So why?

Why, why, why, oh why,
Why has the world gone mad?
Don't they ever have time to think?
Time to stop and change?
Time to just ask.
Why?

Sophie Lamb (11)
Weald CP School

THE SEA

The sea is like the wind blowing somebody over,
The sea is the colour of the sky on a sunny day,
On a rainy day the sea is angry,
On a sunny day the sea is calm,
The sea is as wobbly as a piece of bright blue jelly,
The sea is as pretty as a piece of blue shiny card
                                    on a wall display.

Hannah Whitbourn (9)
Weald CP School

THE OPTI DOP

The Opti Dop was a weird thing,
It had three eyes and two bushy wings,
It had four legs and one arm
And it lived in a bucket on the farm.

The Opti Dop was a weird thing,
It went around with a bell that went ding, ding.
It went to school which was in Poole,
And it climbed over the school's ten foot wall.

The Opti Dop was a weird thing,
It had a great voice with which it could sing.
He joined the choir in the church,
And he sat on a gigantic perch.
The Opti Dop was a weird thing.

William Fauchon-Jones (10)
Weald CP School

NEW BOY

Here I stand all alone,
No one to talk to or play with.
Here I stand all alone,
In the corner on my own.
Here I stand all alone,
Waiting by the telephone.
Here I stand all alone,
alone,
alone,
alone.

Francesca Lee (11)
Weald CP School

MAN ON THE MOON

Jupiter, Saturn, Mars and Pluto,
are,
four planets from space,
Rockets,
Stars,
The sun oh, so hot!
There is Mars riding high in the sky.
Spacecrafts oh who's in there?
My sister thinks there is a man on the moon
Do you think so?
I asked her what he looked like,
She said he had:
Two big eyes,
One big nose,
Three toes,
It has very scruffy hair, she said.

Jupiter and Saturn who is coming to see you next?

Laura Virgo (11)
Weald CP School

THE WIND IS LIKE A ...

The wind is like an Olympic runner
Zooming past the post.
The wind is like a sandstorm
whirling through they are.
The wind is like cold water.
The inside is a whirlpool of cold air.
The wind is a whisper of secrets to the trees.
The wind is a cheetah chasing an antelope.

Samuel Jones (8)
Weald CP School

AMBITION

A vet is what I want to be,
And animals are what I'll care for.
A chameleon is my favourite animal,
For it changes colour,
And it's a mammal.

A tail is what I like to see,
Not broken or bent without any sense,
Just a tail that wants to be shaken.
Two eyes, a nose, a mouth and a head,
Are just what you need to eat with.
No clothes, just fur or scales or feathers on your back,
To keep you warm in the winter.

If I was an animal I would swim very far,
In a light blue ocean following a star.
That's what I would be,
A dolphin in the sea.

Susannah Martin (10)
Weald CP School

MONSTERS

There's a lot more to monsters than people think.
They're not just bloodsucking, flesh eating,
eyeball mashing head creaking beasts.
They live in your attic and under your bed.
There's one in the fridge, or that's what my brother said.
They chew holes in my socks,
Some of them look like rocks.
That is what monsters do.

Christopher Jones (11)
Weald CP School

DESERT

Running through the desert,
Not a drink in sight.
Now I see a fountain,
Oh it's disappeared.
It must have been a mirage,
What an awful shame.
Now I'm thirsty,
Now I'm tired,
I must rest again.

Creeping through the rainforest,
Oh it is so hot.
How I wish I could be home sleeping in the freezer.
Tired and weary.
Oh so weak,
Missing all my family
Now I wake, what a dream.
Lovely to be home.

Helen Smart (11)
Weald CP School

THE SUN

Hmm - the sun is like a big yellow beach ball going round
And round the world,
Like a firework that never seems to burst.
Someone's big cracking bonfire,
And to think someday it will go pop!

Christopher Ryan (10)
Weald CP School

OUTSIDE

The mist thickened,
The snow stopped,
The atmosphere was thin,
The air was silent.

The flowers were covered head to toe,
in snow, snow, snow, snow.
My voice echoed,
Then I froze.

It is cold out here,
my fingers are blue.
There was snow on the edge of the leaves,
where the robins sat.

I came back in,
and tore off my coat,
I sat by the roaring fire,
until I disappeared.

Eleanor Jones (11)
Weald CP School

CIVIL WAR

I can feel boiling hot flowing lead
flow through the back of my neck.
My friend feels his body carved to make arrows.
There I feel cold balls of lead load into the back of me.
Now finally I have been lit to make me fire
(*Bang*) balls of lead fire to the other side of the field.

James Stout (10)
Weald CP School

JIM

There was once a boy who's name was Jim
and he was rather dim.
He picked his nose,
he picked his toes,
so he was rather grim.
He was a shorty
and very naughty.
He scribbled on his work,
he was a berk.

He made a fuss,
while sick on a bus.
He was fired from his job,
so he had a sob!

James Dennison (10)
Weald CP School

UBF

I've got a UBF,
He's so small that you can hardly see him.
I peer down at him and boom 'Hi,'
He has a nose except it's all spotty and red.
He also has nits in his hair, he only washes it once.
He has never had a haircut, his mum does it for him.
His clothes are all baggy, his jeans have a hole in it.
His T-shirt's all muddy,
But I don't care because he is my . . .
    Ugly Best Friend!

Mary Griffiths (11)
Weald CP School

Winter

It was in the bleak midwinter
my feet crunched through the frosty ground
walking through the woods, I could hear not a sound,
a wonderful sight of snowtopped trees
when puddles all over the wood again begin to freeze.

Birds are deep in their nests, squirrels in hibernation.
There was a lovely atmosphere.
Winter, a splendid creation.
Dreaming of wonderful spring snowmen
standing, watching, waiting.

Robert Stone (11)
Weald CP School

Hidden Treasures

I struggled to see some activity
In a small enclosed circle of palm trees
And spied a small, perfect, gold sphere
Like a golden sea
Covering the sun's core
At the last stage of time.

I scanned ever so carefully
Through the dense undergrowth
And found a small container
Decorated with brass and bronze
Like a shiny block
In the blazing sun's rays.

Samuel Holyhead (9)
West Malling CE Primary School

HIDDEN TREASURES

Carefully I peeked in a dusty old box
and glimpsed a chest of golden treasure
like silver fishes in the deep blue sea.

In the corner of my eye
I spotted a stained glass window
I peered and caught sight of an old man crying
like an old lady sighing.

Chantelle Capeling (9)
West Malling CE Primary School

HIDDEN TREASURE

Quietly I stared into a hole
and glimpsed with fright
a tiger
like a ball of fire,
recklessly shooting from the sun.

I spied with caution out of the door,
and encountered bravely
a giant, standing
like a skyscraper in a big city.

Ryan Webb (9)
West Malling CE Primary School

HIDDEN TREASURES

Excitedly, I peeped into a bird box and discovered,
A fragile robin's egg
like a china ball waiting to break
on the coldest day of winter.

Carefully I peered through my binoculars
and glimpsed
a squirrel
like a duster swiftly sweeping itself up the tree
In the autumn.

Jade Thompson (9)
West Malling CE Primary School

IN THE CAVE

I suspiciously looked into the deserted deep dark cave,
But could see nothing but complete and utter darkness,
like at about 9 o'clock on a pitch-black cold winter's night.

I stared into the gloominess
and something caught the corner of my eye.
It was something shimmering
like a crystal in the summer's brightness.

Rebecca Burr (10)
West Malling CE Primary School

HIDDEN TREASURES

Hastily I peeped under a tiny jagged stone
and with amazement I discovered
A slimy worm,
like a butterfly flying through the thin air
on a hot summer's day.

Cautiously I peeped out of the tiny stone and found
A rainbow shining over the hills and houses
like a flutter of raindrops
just waiting to drop off.

Alexandra Gridley (10)
West Malling CE Primary School

HIDDEN TREASURES

As I peeped with curiosity
into an old deserted room
I saw with amazement beyond my wildest dream
A glinting key
on a dusty damp windowsill,
like a rainbow shining over the most vast,
desolate part of the earth.
It lay untouched in the sunlight.

I looked through the decayed window
where the key lay
and saw,
a sly magpie hunting around for gold
and other shiny things,
like a burglar silently robbing a house,
the magpie hunted for those wonderful treasures.

Samantha James (10)
West Malling CE Primary School

HIDDEN TREASURE

Painstakingly I peered over a rock
and glimpsed with happiness
a nest of fluffy birds
like lots of dusters of thistledown
frozen in ice
in shimmering snow.

Prudently I glanced through a brilliant window
and caught sight of
a guinea pig
like a floss of orange fur in the luminous sun.

Christina Theophanides (9)
West Malling CE Primary School

HIDDEN TREASURES

Quickly I gazed on into
A lovely shaped bush
And glimpsed the beautiful colour of the butterflies.
They flapped their wings
Like sparkly gems
With a shiny diamond.

Cautiously I glared through
A round curly vine
And mysteriously stared at
A butterfly's face.
It was like a reindeer's silvery tear
Which dropped on a golden leaf
With a gentle touch
And a splashy fall
To the green and grassy ground.

Azim Sobrany (10)
West Malling CE Primary School

HIDDEN TREASURE

I gazed under a coral reef
In the shimmering sea and came across
A box of gold and silver
Glinting in the sunlight
Like golden hair reflecting the sun's rays
On a beautiful day.

I peeped curiously in a damp and dusty cave
And found a bright shocking
Whirl of white ghost
Like a lifeless skeleton with no bones.

Joshua de Gray (9)
West Malling CE Primary School

HIDDEN TREASURES

Cautiously I peered under a yellow leaf,
and spied a wriggly caterpillar
like wobbly balls of green bubblegum
stuck together,
struggling to escape,
from each other's grips.

Dreamily I gazed out of a window
and saw a tree,
dancing about with the wind flowing
through its long branches,
like a calm sea,
moving slowly up to the shore of a vast
and desolate beach.

Sammi-Jo Lawrence (10)
West Malling CE Primary School

MY HIDDEN TREASURES

I gazed cautiously
into the sparkly sea and
glimpsed suddenly
a fish
like a shiny rainbow coloured gem in the sea.

Sneakily I glared
through the window
and caught mysteriously
in the corner of my eye
a lizard like golden raindrops
splattering on the silver framed window.

Jake Smith (9)
West Malling CE Primary School

HIDDEN TREASURES

Nervously I peeped down a dusty cellar
and stared at
an old beer bottle shining like a rainbow
being burnt to the ground
on the coldest day in summer.

Carefully I peered out of a wet car window
and saw
an old lady taking her grandchildren to school
in the cold misty rain
like a lollipop lady
helping the children cross the busy bumpy road
on the coldest day in winter.

Deanne Soules (10)
West Malling CE Primary School

HIDDEN TREASURES

Warily I spied under my bed
and discovered with surprise
a golden parrot
like a juicy ripe peach
on a tropical tree in the luscious jungle.

Dreamingly I gazed into the deep sparkling sea
and sighted with fright,
a ferocious shark
like a silver sword
being swung by a brave knight.

Marcus Towner (10)
West Malling CE Primary School

HIDDEN TREASURES

Curiously I peered
In a steel container
And quickly discovered
A beautiful painting
Like a swan swimming down a river
On a winter's day.

I stared carefully through
A pair of rusty binoculars
And focused and tracked a swift
Skimming the clear blue sky
Like a jet engine that never ran out of fuel
And had not a care in the world.

Ben Greenwood (10)
West Malling CE Primary School

HIDDEN TREASURES

Cautiously, I examined a mound of earth
and cast my eye on,
a tarantula,
like a man's scruffy beard,
on the day of the universe's bad hair day.

Quietly I peered through a dug up hole
and discovered
a rabbit
like a ball of wool
from your Gran's knitting basket.

Katherine Styance (9)
West Malling CE Primary School